Teaching Good Behavior

By the Editors of Time-Life Books

Alexandria, Virginia

TIME LIFE BOOKS®

Time-Life Books Inc.
is a wholly owned subsidiary of

Time Incorporated

FOUNDER: Henry R. Luce 1898-1967

Editor-in-Chief: Henry Anatole Grunwald
Chairman and Chief Executive Officer:
J. Richard Munro
President and Chief Operating Officer:
N. J. Nicholas Jr.
Chairman of the Executive Committee:
Ralph P. Davidson
Corporate Editor: Ray Cave
Executive Vice President, Books: Kelso F. Sutton
Vice President, Books: George Artandi

Time-Life Books Inc.

EDITOR: George Constable
Executive Editor: Ellen Phillips
Director of Design: Louis Klein
Director of Editorial Resources: Phyllis K. Wise
Editorial Board: Russell B. Adams Jr., Dale M.
Brown, Roberta Conlan, Thomas H. Flaherty,
Lee Hassig, Donia Ann Steele, Rosalind Stubenberg,
Kit van Tulleken, Henry Woodhead
Director of Photography and Research:
John Conrad Weiser

PRESIDENT: Christopher T. Linen
Chief Operating Officer: John M. Fahey Jr.
Senior Vice Presidents: James L. Mercer,
Leopoldo Toralballa
Vice Presidents: Stephen L. Bair, Ralph J. Cuomo,
Neal Goff, Stephen L. Goldstein, Juanita T. James,
Hallett Johnson III, Carol Kaplan, Susan J. Maruyama,
Robert H. Smith, Paul R. Stewart, Joseph J. Ward
Director of Production Services:
Robert J. Passantino

Library of Congress Cataloguing in
Publication Data
Teaching good behavior.
   (Successful parenting)
   Bibliography: p.
   Includes index.
   1. Child rearing. 2. Parent and child.
3. Discipline of children. I. Time-Life Books. II.
Series.
HQ769.T397 1987   649'.64   87-10000
ISBN 0-8094-5933-7
ISBN 0-8094-5934-5 (lib. bdg.)

Successful Parenting

SERIES DIRECTOR: Donia Ann Steele
Deputy Editor: Dale M. Brown
Series Administrator: Norma E. Shaw
Editorial Staff for *Teaching Good Behavior:*
Designer: Raymond Ripper
Picture Editor: Blaine Marshall
Text Editor: Robert A. Doyle
Staff Writer: Charlotte Anker
Researchers: Fran Moshos, Nancy C. Scott
(principals), Karen Monks, Mark Moss
Assistant Designer: Susan M. Gibas
Copy Coordinator: Marfé Ferguson
Picture Coordinator: Linda Yates
Editorial Assistant: Jenester C. Lewis

Special Contributors: Laura Akgulian, Amy Aldrich,
George Daniels, Marilyn Humm, Christine Lyons,
Wendy Murphy (text); Ann Muñoz-Furlong,
(research)

Editorial Operations
Copy Chief: Diane Ullius
Editorial Operations Manager: Caroline A. Boubin
Production: Celia Beattie
Quality Control: James J. Cox (director)
Library: Louise D. Forstall

Correspondents: Elisabeth Kraemer-Singh (Bonn);
Maria Vincenza Aloisi (Paris); Ann Natanson
(Rome). Valuable assistance was also provided by:
Christina Lieberman (New York).

First printing. Printed in U.S.A.

Published simultaneously in Canada.
School and library distribution by
Silver Burdett Company, Morristown,
New Jersey 07960.

TIME-LIFE is a trademark of Time
Incorporated U.S.A.

Other Publications

MYSTERIES OF THE UNKNOWN
TIME FRAME
FIX IT YOURSELF
FITNESS, HEALTH & NUTRITION
HEALTHY HOME COOKING
UNDERSTANDING COMPUTERS
LIBRARY OF NATIONS
THE ENCHANTED WORLD
THE KODAK LIBRARY OF CREATIVE PHOTOGRAPHY
GREAT MEALS IN MINUTES
THE CIVIL WAR
PLANET EARTH
COLLECTOR'S LIBRARY OF THE CIVIL WAR
THE EPIC OF FLIGHT
THE GOOD COOK
WORLD WAR II
HOME REPAIR AND IMPROVEMENT
THE OLD WEST

*For information on and a full description
of any of the Time-Life Books series listed
above, please write:*
Reader Information
Time-Life Customer Service
P.O. Box C-32068
Richmond, Virginia 23261-2068

This volume is one of a series about raising children.

The Consultants

General Consultants

Dr. Rex Forehand, a clinical psychologist and leading authority on the assessment and treatment of behavior problems in preschool children, is research professor of psychology and director of the Center for Family Research at the University of Georgia at Athens. He is currently studying the effects of marital conflict, divorce, depression and other parental disorders on the behavior of young children and adolescents. Dr. Forehand has written or co-authored more than a hundred articles and book chapters on childhood behavior issues. He is the author of *Helping the Noncompliant Child: A Clinician's Guide to Effective Parent Training.*

Dr. Victoria V. Lavigne, a clinical psychologist, is president and executive director of Tuesday's Child, a program that teaches parenting skills to families who have experienced difficulties in managing the behavior of their children aged 18 months to five years. She is also a consultant to public and private nursery schools and day-care centers on the subject of discipline. Dr. Lavigne is currently an assistant professor of clinical psychiatry and pediatrics at Northwestern University Medical School in Chicago.

Special Consultants

Dr. Edward R. Christophersen, who gave his expert view on the question of obtaining professional help for behavior problems, is a professor of pediatrics at the University of Kansas Medical Center in Kansas City. In addition, Dr. Christophersen runs a behavioral pediatrics practice in which he works with parents and children on discipline and other family issues. He has written widely on the subject of improving parent-child interactions and is editorial consultant to *The Parenting Advisor.*

Dr. Willard W. Hartup, professor of child psychology at the Institute of Child Development at the University of Minnesota in Minneapolis, assisted with the chapter on peer relationships. He is a pioneer in this field and is the author of several major works on the subject. The editor of *Child Development,* Dr. Hartup is currently engaged in research on children's friendships. Previously he has written on such problems as dependency, aggression, sex-role preferences and peer pressures in the social development of children.

Dr. Thomas Lickona, who contributed to the developmental essay in the first chapter of *Teaching Good Behavior,* is an international authority on moral development in children and a past president of the Association for Moral Education. A professor of education at the State University of New York at Cortland, Dr. Lickona is a frequent speaker at conferences for parents and teachers, as well as a guest on television and radio talk shows across the country. He is the author of *Raising Good Children,* which describes the stages of moral development from birth through the teenage years.

Dr. Robert B. McCall, professor of psychology and director of the Office of Child Development at the University of Pittsburgh, wrote the expert's box on spanking. He is a frequent consultant on child behavior to teachers, legislators and social service professionals. He serves on the editorial board of several psychology journals and is a contributing editor of *Parents* magazine, where he writes the monthly "About Fathers" column.

Contents

4 Getting Along with Others 92

5 Putting Good Discipline to Work 118

The ABC's of Good Behavior

If there is one desire that virtually all mothers and fathers share, it is the wish to raise a good child. But ask any dozen parents to define "good" and you are bound to get a dozen different answers. One parent cares strongly about manners and politeness — the kinds of behaviors the youngsters opposite are practicing so earnestly at an imaginary tea party. Another will cite responsibility and obedience to family rules as the essence of virtue. A third parent upholds self-control and cooperativeness as the most admirable of character traits, and a fourth emphasizes ethical conduct — such qualities as honesty, kindness and trustworthiness. But in truth, good behavior is all these things and more, and given the proper opportunity, your youngster will be able to make all of them part of his own character.

As a loving parent, what strategies can you use to encourage character building? For one thing, you can give your child abundant reasons to trust you and to feel secure in your care. For another, you can be a good role model, demonstrating the values and behaviors you want him to adopt. You can also set reasonable limits and positive expectations, appropriate to his age and temperament. You can be a firm, fair, consistent and loving disciplinarian without resorting to harsh punishment. And you can help him find his way within the larger community of friends, school and strangers — explaining, interpreting, guiding and lending a sympathetic ear as he meets each new social challenge. But you cannot make your child be good: That, in the end, is up to him.

A Portrait of the Well-Behaved Child

What qualities distinguish the well-behaved child? He is, in essence, a good citizen — a young person who has a healthy sense of self, who gets along well with family and friends, who has the inner resources and the self-control needed to regulate his actions in the world at large. But such a child does not simply happen; he is the product of a long learning process, one that begins in the earliest days of life and continues throughout the years of childhood.

Babies and young children are totally self-centered in their outlook on life, light-years away from understanding the needs of others or the moral principles of right and wrong. As experienced parents know well, it takes years of patient and steady work to impose civilizing restraints on a little one's natural impulses and to teach him the behaviors that will enable him to get along in the big world beyond the nursery.

The importance of love

What babies and young children understand best is the unstinting love of their parents — and of the many foundation stones of good behavior, parental love is surely the greatest. At the outset, it gives your helpless infant the sense of security he needs to develop trust in the world and in other people. Being on the receiving end of love and affection teaches the child to express his own loving feelings in turn and, ultimately, opens the door to healthy social relationships with others.

As the child grows older, the abiding love of his mother and father also gives him the feeling that he is special, a person worthy of regard, thus building in him a reservoir of self-esteem. Child-development experts agree that high self-esteem is a vital prerequisite to good behavior, as well as to overall social and emotional adjustment throughout life. The youngster who feels good about himself has a much greater incentive to behave well — in effect, to live up to his reputation — than the child who does not have such a positive self-image of himself to maintain.

Although young children are self-centered by nature, they should be taught at an early age to respect the feelings and needs of others — as this little boy is doing in gently checking on his sleeping baby sister.

Respect for the feelings of others

Out of the loving bond with his parents grows another important characteristic of the well-behaved child: the realization that his mother and father and the other people in his life have feelings and needs just as he does, and that he must respect others' feelings in order to get along in society. It takes years for a young child to comprehend fully how his actions impinge on other people — that through his behavior, for example, he can make a friend feel happy or sad.

During the preschool years he may be incapable of true empathy — a personal identification with the hurts, fears and joys of those around him. But at the very least he can be taught to respect the feelings of those he comes into direct contact with, including the family pet. Although he may have difficulties with many of the social niceties for a long time, he will benefit greatly from having the right rules in place early and from being rewarded with praise whenever he is thoughtful toward the people around him.

With a sense of accomplishment, a toddler brings in the morning newspaper while his father holds open the door for him. Such small tasks build responsibility and pride in the very young.

Responsibility and cooperation

The awareness that there is more to life than the gratification of needs leads to a sense of responsibility, another key foundation stone of good behavior. Of the many social limits that your child must absorb in her preschool years, the most basic is responsibility for her own physical and emotional actions. She must come to recognize that such aggressive acts as hitting and pushing are not acceptable ways of dealing with frustrations, and that to get along with others she will need to share, take turns and cooperate in group activities.

Responsible behavior should also include the concept of cooperating and sharing the work load at home. Even at the toddler stage, having a few simple duties such as putting stuffed animals away on their shelf at bedtime will help give your child the proud feeling that she is an important member of the family.

A third aspect of responsibility is respect for property and place. The well-behaved child recognizes the difference between things that are rightfully hers and those that are not. As she learns about ownership, her evolving sense of responsibility will keep her from taking another child's toy without asking or from carelessly handling an object that does not belong to her.

Along the same lines, the youngster can be made to appreciate that the environment both inside and outside the home deserves her respect, too.

Respect for rules A character trait that goes hand in hand with responsible social behavior is an individual's willingness to play by the rules — whether they are imposed by parents, nursery school teachers or society at large. Over the years, guidelines for your child's conduct will range all the way from, "No-no, stove hot!" to the more abstract moral laws against lying, cheating and stealing.

At the toddler and preschool stage, of course, children are not yet emotionally and mentally mature enough to grasp the loftier social standards of fairness, honesty, trustworthiness, forgiveness, humility and courage. Nonetheless, if a child is to grow up in harmony with the world around her, she must begin learning to follow rules at a tender age. In the earliest years the child will benefit if rules are kept as simple and clear as possible, with allowances made for the many missteps that are bound to occur along the way. In time, as the youngster develops more mature reasoning powers, she will understand the basis for the rules that you have taught her to follow, and the lapses should be fewer.

Independence of mind While the good child will display a healthy respect for rules and for the authority that lies behind them, goodness should never be equated with mindless obedience. On the contrary, strength of character includes the ability to think and make decisions independently. A youngster should have enough confidence in his own judgment, for example, that in years to come he will be able to resist negative peer pressures and make his own positive choices instead.

As a parent, you can foster such independence early on by giving your little one freedom to make simple choices — such as the red sweater instead of the blue one, or peas rather than carrots for dinner. This will help build his confidence in his ability to manage things for himself and will encourage him to view himself as a competent, successful person.

A child works at a construction toy, learning by trial and error how to piece it together. The reward for his persistence is the finished structure — as well as his mother's lavish praise.

Old-fashioned stick-to-itiveness — the willingness to keep trying in the face of discouragement — is another sturdy virtue that parents should begin nurturing early. The ability to solve difficult problems and master new challenges contributes mightily to healthy feelings of independence in a growing child. Persistence also increases a child's chances of succeeding at the task of the moment — and of all positive incentives, nothing works better than success.

Whenever your child is struggling to accomplish a new task, you should make a point of praising his diligent efforts as much as the good results. He will benefit, too, from being allowed to work at his own pace, in the knowledge that help is at hand if he needs it.

Perseverance, it should be noted, is a quality that parents themselves will need in steady supply over the course of raising children from infancy to adulthood. Your child's progress toward the good behavior goals you have set for him will undoubtedly occur in fits and starts, with backslidings, and you may find yourself still grappling with some behavior issues when your youngster is old enough to leave home. But in the long view, the rewards are well worth the effort: No parental legacy is more important to your child's lifelong happiness and success than the social values and living skills you begin teaching in early childhood. ❖

A group of kindergartners obey a crossing guard who will wave them across the intersection when all traffic has stopped. Such experiences teach youngsters respect for rules, a fundamental principle of good behavior.

Parental Attitudes and Actions

The word "discipline" means different things to different people. In its best sense the term describes a positive, pervasive form of life training aimed at the development and reinforcement of good behavior. In its narrowest sense, it stands for punishment, involving a range of mild to harsh penalties imposed after specific displeasing acts.

In their efforts to determine how such positive characteristics as self-control, self-worth, cooperativeness and socialization evolve in children, child specialists describe the diverse styles of discipline practiced by modern American parents in one of three ways: authoritarian, permissive and authoritative. Probably no parent uses a pure form of any one of these; most mothers and fathers waffle to some degree as a result of conflicts between their upbringing and their philosophy, or perhaps between their rational intentions and their emotions. All parents, too, are subject to moods and frustrations that distort their reactions or color their feelings at any given time. Furthermore, the child's own temperament, as discussed on pages 16-17, brings modifications both in the way she accepts discipline and in the way parents administer it. But in broad outline, experts describe the characteristics and effects of the three prevailing styles of discipline as follows.

The authoritarian style
Authoritarian discipline casts the parent as boss and the child as someone who must obey. At an extreme, authoritarian parents consider obedience a virtue in its own right. They lay down rules, rarely explain why the rules are to be followed or how they reflect parental values, and give no quarter to exceptions. Pure authoritarians seldom encourage their child's opinions on issues of discipline, apparently in the belief that to permit the youngster some say in the matter would be a sign of parental weakness or uncertainty. Their assumption is that the child would prefer to be childish and irresponsible.

Because they regard their power as absolute, authoritarian parents tend to see punishment as a way of reminding the child who is in charge, and in that context a spanking, which promotes the youngster's sense of helplessness and submission, is more often than not the punishment of choice. Other authoritarian parents will punish by withdrawing themselves from their children, holding back their love until the desired effect is achieved. But many disciplinarians of this type simply supervise their children so closely that punishment is rarely necessary at all; the restrictions they impose preclude misbehavior.

Authoritarianism, ironically, seldom produces the highly disciplined personality that the parents aim for. Children raised too strictly tend to follow parental rules out of fear, rather than out of respect for the essential rightness of the rules. They learn to accept punishment as full payment for mischief; the only regret they are likely to feel is that they were caught misbehaving. Boys in particular exhibit a tendency to become hostile as a result of this type of upbringing.

Having never been given reasons for the restrictions continually imposed upon them, children of authoritarian parents show little motivation to internalize good behavior and fail to understand how their own actions affect others. Such children have a hard time making decisions, and they are often stunted in their intellectual curiosity and creativity, since their imaginations have been effectively stifled.

Many children of authoritarian parents grow up feeling that their thoughts and feelings count for little, and as a result, they suffer from low self-esteem. When they reach adolescence, they have difficulty turning to their parents for support because no lines of communication have been established. Those who are naturally shy may feel helpless and anxious, while the more aggressive individuals may begin to act out their hostility toward their parents and society.

The permissive style   Parents given to an overly permissive style of discipline, by contrast, are child-centered, warm and indulgent to the point of rarely exercising any discipline at all. They believe that the child's impulses and desires are good merely by virtue of being natural, and they hope that in allowing the child to express her instincts she will eventually modify her behavior for the better out of her own free will. They fear that the assertion of parental values will thwart the youngster's emotional development; they prefer to avoid even mild punishment, out of concern that it will undermine the bonds of love. They tend to see themselves as the exemplars of the behavior they would like their children to adopt.

There is no doubt that the love of such parents for their children is real and that the youngsters revel in it. But mothers and fathers who let their indulgence get out of hand often wind up with the classic spoiled brat — a child whose noncompliant behavior negatively colors her relationships with people outside the family circle and leaves her at odds with herself. Having never had limits put upon her at home, she can hardly be expected to impose them on herself when she ventures into the world at large. By failing to help her to get along with others and by neglecting to prepare her for the give-and-take world that lies beyond the family, the parents have unwittingly left their beloved child open to a rude awakening.

In cases where the parents are too busy or too preoccupied to do anything but give in to their child, the youngster often becomes emotionally insecure. Without the external restraints she needs to give some structure to her life, she feels very vulnerable: An anything-goes policy simply gives a young child more freedom and power than her immature psyche is equipped to handle. Sometimes, when her uncontrolled emotions erupt into tantrums and bouts of destructiveness, the youngster can actually frighten herself.

Some children respond to a lack of parental involvement by running wild and becoming aggressive, self-centered and irresponsible, as if to force their parents to pay attention to them at last through intervention of some sort. Others deal with their vulnerability by becoming extremely timid or clinging, avoiding opportunities for experimentation and self-expression.

The authoritative style

The third discipline style, and — in the majority view of child experts — the one that proves most successful, is authoritative as opposed to authoritarian. It is variously characterized as being trusting, relaxed and democratic. In many ways it represents a middle-of-the-road position, in which parents set high standards for their child's behavior, are quick to give approval when the youngster achieves reasonable compliance and are equally

Teaching responsibility, a mother shows her daughter how to put away toys. She will repeat the act with the child until the youngster learns to do it on her own. A good job will earn praise; forgetfulness will bring firm but patient reminders.

quick to provide firm but fair correction by way of punishment when he transgresses the rules.

Unlike the kinds of penalties that authoritarian parents favor, authoritative punishments tend to be reasonable and logical consequences of the misbehavior. Ideally, they work to teach the child something useful about the value of good behavior, and they are mild enough that the child can still have room in his feelings for remorse.

Authoritative parents also spend considerable time explaining the reasons behind rules, so that their child gradually comes to understand and respect the values the rules represent. Once a child shows some readiness to adopt a desired behavior, his parents offer encouragement and provide him opportunities to practice the new skill. After he has shown mastery of the behavior they then pull back, to let him know they trust him to carry it out. In the process his self-esteem grows.

Underlying the philosophy of authoritative discipline is the assumption that children are eager to be good if only someone will show them how. Authoritative parents accept as a given that the developing child will err frequently. They see this occurring not out of willful misbehavior from the child or from some failure on their part, but because the young one has not yet learned priorities and has many conflicting needs that want servicing simultaneously. Such mothers and fathers are prepared to be patient, to repeat many tiresome lessons over and over, and to resist the temptation to take the easy, indulgent — indeed, lazy — shortcut. They are open-minded, as willing to learn from their children as teach them. They believe that each member of the family has rights and responsibilities, and that in consistent, effective discipline all parties can flourish.

The weight of evidence seems to bear this out. Children of authoritative parents are more apt to be assertive, self-reliant and achievement-oriented, and better able to cooperate and get along with others. Because they have been well loved and treated firmly but fairly by their own parents, they tend to trust and are themselves trustworthy. And because they understand not just the letter of their parents' law but the spirit and reason behind it, they do well when it comes to making moral choices and are effective exemplars and teachers of that law.

Moreover, as long-range studies have shown, when youngsters raised this way grow up and become parents themselves, they tend to treat their offspring in the same firm, fair and loving manner, thus passing on the gifts and rewards of good discipline to another generation. ∴

A Matter of Temperament

Children's temperaments are as varied as spring flowers. Even when parents subscribe wholeheartedly to the tenets of authoritative discipline, their child's basic temperament may require them to modify their modes of discipline.

Temperament has to do with the way a child is physiologically and psychologically equipped to react to her world and the challenges in it — her internal levels of nervous arousal, excitability, anxiety. You have only to consider how different the behavior and character of siblings can be, even though the same set of parental rules have been applied to each, to recognize the influences that individual personality exerts on behavior.

Child specialists recognize and identify three basic categories of temperament among children: easy, quiet and difficult. The descriptions of temperament that follow are broadly drawn to take into account the specific traits each type exhibits; you may find that your child displays some traits from all three.

The easy child   Children with easy temperaments adapt with little trouble to new schedules, new faces, new foods. They tend to react to novelty with a minimum of fussing, and they generally raise short-lived protests when something does trouble them. They have relatively cheerful dispositions, are regular in their sleep, eating and digestive functions, and do not become frustrated easily. Lucky is the parent who has an easy youngster, for that child is likely to take authoritative discipline with good grace and to learn readily from its lessons.

The quiet child   Highly sensitive, the quiet child is prone to feelings of discomfort in new situations, even with a parent present. Such a youngster should be handled somewhat more gently than the easy child. If she feels pressured to adopt unfamiliar behaviors more quickly than her temperament allows, her way of coping may be to withdraw, suck her thumb or quietly cry. Parents who respond by trying to force the issue, either through badgering or punish-

The easy child is quick to make new friends and to join in cooperative play. Here, two boys are having a go at the sand table, agreeably sharing a sifter.

The quiet child very much needs time and space to do things her own way, at her own pace. Parents can stimulate greater sociability by gently encouraging her tentative overtures to others.

ment, are likely to send the child into even deeper withdrawal or to trigger stubborn resistance that puts everyone at odds. It is thus better to show patience in the face of these realities, presenting the same requirement a few times without criticizing the child for her failure to accept them; in most cases she will yield in her own time.

The difficult child   Characterized by the unpredictability of his sleeping, eating and waking habits, the difficult youngster cries frequently and lustily, is quickly frustrated and smiles less easily and less often than other youngsters his age. He has tantrums when things do not go exactly his way, and he takes considerably longer to adjust to new experiences than less intense children.

In disciplining the difficult child, parents might as well decide at the outset to adjust their expectations somewhat. They should never lose sight of their goals but move with persistence toward them. Trying to go against the grain, to make the youngster calm and compliant, will just end up in frustration for all. Once he has been the recipient of too many punishments, the child knows that he cannot please and loses interest in trying to do many of the things his parents require. Hitting and throwing all too often turn out to be his way of coping with a discouraging situation.

Child behavior experts recommend that parents of difficult children simplify their demands and prohibitions. This may well mean setting priorities, putting such all-important issues as safety at the very top of the must list. Also important is getting the child to modify his aggression against people and things. And you may have to defer such niceties as table manners and neatness until later if he puts up resistance. Above all, parents of difficult children need to display patience, firmness and consistency in handling disciplinary matters. Mothers and fathers who keep trying new approaches to behavior control only make matters worse by being indulgent one day and strict the next; the overreactive child is likely to recognize this as a power struggle and to escalate it.

Whatever your own child's temperament, as you evolve your individual disciplining style, pay close attention to his reactions and pace your demands accordingly. When you accept him for the individual he is and become his partner rather than his adversary in discipline, you will allow his strengths to develop and his natural potentials to come to the fore. ❖

The difficult child is often easy to spot in a crowd. Like this little girl, she is the one who moves more, makes more noise, creates more disruptions and frazzles more nerves than all the other youngsters. But her energy can be delightful, too.

Learning to Be Good

Anyone who has seen a child through the child-rearing process knows that youngsters cannot be rushed into good conduct. A child's readiness to behave in socially acceptable ways depends on many factors, including her innate temperament, the degree to which she senses that she is loved and how much she wishes to please her parents. But even when these factors are positive, no child can be expected to behave any better than her developing intellect and emotions will allow at the moment.

Does this mean that you should ignore bad behavior while you wait for your daughter or son to display the first signs of moral awareness? Certainly not. Misbehavior at any stage of development can become the seed of troublesome and enduring habits if parents simply allow it to continue. Parents who give in to demanding behavior from their year-old toddler will face many more tantrums and manipulations than parents who do not give in. So you have every reason to want to shape your child's attitudes, no matter how young she is. But in doing so you must be responsive to what is — or is not — possible at her particular age.

Consider the actions of your rambunctious two-year-old, for example. You cannot expect her to understand fully the notion of private property. When you find her routinely taking candy or gum off store shelves as you shop, it does neither of you any good if you think of her as stealing, which implies a considered act well beyond her cognitive abilities at this stage. She can, on the other hand, distinguish between "yours" and "mine"; in fact, "mine" is often a two-year-old's favorite word. It would be appropriate for you to tell her, "No, not yours," in a firm but calm voice, put the candy back and give her a permissible substitute to hold. If you find your three-year-old doing the same thing, you can and should say more about the reasons why taking candy is not allowed. By this age, children have a rudimentary sense of right and wrong and will feel some remorse at doing wrong; they can profit from a fuller explanation of why an action such as taking someone else's things is not acceptable behavior.

The essay on the following pages traces the general course of moral and social development that children undergo in their preschool years. Bear in mind that children differ in their rates of growth; just as some youngsters are early talkers, some learn sooner to follow rules. The actions you take will certainly influence your child's behavior at every stage of development, but at some stages it will be easier to teach the behavior you would like to see than at others. Knowing what children are like at different developmental levels will help you understand that some of the problems are part of normal growth. Progress will also be uneven: Within the same developmental stage, your child may alternate between times when she is cooperative, expansive and socially secure and periods when she is rebellious, insecure and emotionally off balance. All this is a natural part of her journey toward self-control.

Birth to 18 Months

For the first few weeks of his life, the baby is busy during his waking hours trying to gain some grip on his body and his environment, and he is far from being ready for even the simplest lessons in behavior. But this is when the foundations of good behavior are laid, through the love and security his parents provide and the hugs, kisses and smiles they bestow on him for even the smallest of his achievements. As the baby grows secure in this loving attachment, he learns to trust his mother and father and to seek their approval, and this will facilitate teaching good behavior.

Soon the early attachment between the baby and his parents is fortified by an exchanging of smiles, gestures and vocalizations. By the time the baby is two months old, he probably will have begun to smile in response to his parents' faces and voices. If his mother leans over and makes cooing sounds, the baby is likely to imitate her and coo back. By the time the child is three to four months of age, parents can stimulate extended interactions of this kind. Soon the baby will be initiating these exchanges.

In these ways, a baby is beginning to develop two crucial social abilities: imitation and reciprocity. Most of the positive social behaviors a child learns in the early years — such as sharing, polite manners and taking turns — are developed through imitation. And throughout life, reciprocity — treating others as you would have them treat you — is the essence of social adjustment and the core of morality.

As he grows, a baby gets increasingly better at deriving information from his parents' faces and the faces of others. A look of pleasure signifies "proceed" to him, one of anger says "stop." He is now ready to learn not just from his own experiences but also vicariously, from those he observes you undergoing.

Plainly having fun feeding himself and playing with his food, this one-year-old has no notion of right and wrong, clean and messy. Rather than chide him, his mother has wisely decided to give him a big bib and let him enjoy his meal in his own way.

Between the ages of six and nine months, babies come to understand the basic meaning of "no." However, if they are already engaged in an interesting behavior, such as emptying the flour onto the kitchen floor, a loud "No!" may actually intensify the activity underway. At this age, the reaction is not defiance; it is a natural physical response to the extra excitement caused by your outburst. In such a situation, the best course is to remove your baby from whatever he has gotten into, by moving either him or the object of interest. Between nine months and a year, most babies can understand and comply with simple requests such as: "Come here," "Give it to me," or "Hold still." This gives your child the capacity for his first acts of obedience, an important milestone in learning to behave.

Walking ushers in a new period of independence, exploration and assertiveness — and bouts of frustration when the child finds he cannot go everywhere and have everything he wants. From that frustration spring the first expressions of aggression, often around 15 to 16 months. Many parents are understandably shocked when their adorable baby begins to throw objects and strike out at things — or even at them. While such behavior is a perfectly natural result of the child's development, parents should resolve to stay in control and redirect their toddler toward more appropriate behavior, perhaps by diverting his attention to an activity he can pursue.

18 Months to Three Years

The youngster in the early phases of this growth period begins to make distinctions between "yours" and "mine," to claim "mine" and to resist sharing. At the same time, toddler negativism blossoms into a full-scale declaration of independence. "No" becomes the most common word in a two-year-old's vocabulary: "No dinner!" "No bath!" "No, don't wanna go to bed!" Sometimes defiance is blatant — as, for example, when Daddy announces that there will be no more TV and turns the set off, and the two-year-old, looking his father right in the eye, goes over and turns it back on — watching all the time to see what Daddy will do.

All this resistance and testing is part of the child's pulling away from his parents and becoming his own person. Parents must find ways to respect their youngster's developing independence, while at the same time placing limits on behavior and encouraging cooperation.

Impulse control is weak during this period. A two-year-old can understand that he should not pull the cat's tail or another child's hair because those things hurt. But the fact that he understands the reasons for behaving properly does not mean he will always do so. Try as he might to rein himself in, the child still lacks adequate inner controls; this is why tantrums and physical aggression appear from time to time.

Your toddler needs an environment that is conducive to reasonable behavior. Temptation should not be put in his way; objects that are not to be touched or held should be kept out of his reach. At this stage of his development, distraction usually works better than discipline: Calling attention to the plane in the sky or the flower blooming on the window sill will divert his attention long enough for him to lose interest in the forbidden activity he was pursuing. This does not mean, however, that you should refrain from laying down clear, firm and consistent rules whenever they are needed.

Often unable to differentiate between fantasy and reality, truth and falsehood, the youngster this age firmly believes in magic as an explanation for many events and may think that inanimate objects have the power to punish as surely as people do. Thus, the youngster who bashes his thumb while playing with a forbidden hammer is likely to assume that the hammer has punished him for disobeying. Such beliefs may also lead the child to deny accountability for his actions: When asked if he knocked over the lamp or tracked in the mud, he will typically blame someone or something else. For example, one two-year-old blamed all spills, breakage and assorted messes he created on a little mouse he claimed was living in the house.

But even this reaction is a form of moral progress; it shows that the child is very much aware of his parents' standards for desirable and undesirable behavior. Blaming others is the first step in internalizing these standards; self-criticism — and eventually, self-control — will come later.

Even though children in this period are usually more independent and rebellious than ever before, they have a growing capacity for cooperation and concern for the feelings of others. It may not happen too frequently, but on occasion they will express sympathy, offer helpful suggestions and try to comfort or cheer another child or an adult in distress. Parents should take care not to get so caught up in the struggles of the twos that they fail to elicit, notice and reinforce these first stirrings of empathy in their child — another important prerequisite to social maturity.

In refusing his sandwich, a toddler is exercising the familiar negativism of the two-year-old. His "no" may be a way of asserting independence, and trying to force him to eat will only lead to a fruitless power struggle. Instead his mother should explain the consequences of his behavior: If he does not eat his lunch, he will be hungry later.

Three to Four Years

Having fought the battle for independence at two, three-year-olds change from rebels to joiners; they have broken away, and now they are more willing to go along. A child's mental development to this point has helped her to build ideas of an ordered, predictable world, and she is usually uncomfortable when someone tries to scramble the routines she has come to accept as proper. Threes obey rules more or less by rote and even take pleasure and pride in following them — with exceptions, of course. There will still be plenty of times when you and your child have conflicts. But in general, threes are more cooperative, easier to manage and to reason with.

Advances in comprehension and language development give rise to this new spirit of cooperation; at three, your child is better able to understand your explanations of right and wrong and is more responsive to the spoken word, so that a simple directive from you has a much greater impact than before. Bear in mind, however, that children can be very literal-minded in interpreting others' meanings and may fail to follow orders merely because they have interpreted them differently from what you have intended. If you tell your child to jump in the car, for example, be prepared for an actual leap.

Growth in language skills also enables the child of three to begin to internalize her parents' admonitions and from time to time say "no" to herself. At this stage she is becoming adept at putting social behaviors into "good" and "bad" categories. Hitting and stealing are naughty, for example, while sharing and picking up toys are nice. With her expanding powers of reasoning, she does not need to wait and see which actions get punished or rewarded before applying the appropriate moral label. You can help develop this capacity for judging social behaviors by discussing specific situations with your child: "That's very nice of you to share with Sammy," you might say, or, "Sally did a good job helping you put the blocks away."

The three-year-old's desire to please makes this a good time for developing habits of helping around the house and for teaching simple table manners and other courtesies *(pages 134-139).* When teaching these lessons in responsibility, parents may combine appeals to the child's pride, such as, "You sure are a big help to Mommy," with appeals to her self-interest — for instance, "Since you helped me fold the baby's diapers, I'll have more time to read you a story."

At this stage, imitation is more important than ever as a

This three-year-old is eating dinner out of a muffin pan because she insists that her foods not touch. Rather than force the issue, her mother took the child's normal ritualistic behavior in stride and came up with the idea for the pan.

source of moral learning — another reason why it is important for you and your youngster to do things around the house together. The three-year-old who helps her father plant flowers or her mother bake brownies for the school fair is not only learning specific skills; she is deepening her identification with her parents and her receptivity to their values.

All the while parents are appreciating and building on the major advances made by their three-year-old, they need to keep in mind all the ways in which she is still socially and emotionally immature. Threes have little ability to see things from another person's point of view and therefore may think a frog would make a swell birthday present for Mom. The child this age may get very frustrated and lose control when she has to wait for something or has difficulty accomplishing a task she is attempting, such as building a block tower or making a bed. She is extremely vulnerable to feelings of jealousy — of a new baby sister, for example — and may react aggressively by biting or hitting. She may still throw temper tantrums, as well — although she probably will come out of them sooner than she did at two.

Four to Five Years

The behavior of the typical four-year-old reveals a swing back toward independence. Parents will see a new kind of out-of-bounds behavior aimed at testing the limits: Your child may resist most suggestions, rules and other forms of teaching as incursions on her emerging sense of self and her abilities. You may find that she likes to call names, to brag and quarrel, and perhaps she also savors offensive words, including the ones that have to do with toilet functions. This is all part of the four-year-old's new self-confidence.

In her relations with others, the child at this stage may show a combination of assertiveness and sociability. Sometimes both of these traits will be evident at the same time, as in her eagerness to press you with endless questions.

Highly talkative now, your four-year-old may voice her growing awareness of moral issues — for example, by commenting on the disloyalty, dishonesty or compassion expressed in a fairy tale she has heard. On the other hand, her moral reasoning at this point is likely to be self-centered. She may believe in fairness with ferocity but define fair as getting her way. Where the two-year-old said simply, "I want it," the four-year-old may say, "I want it, and it's not fair if I don't get it." The challenge for parents is to stretch the child's moral judgment to include other points of view. This, of course, is easier to do when the child is calm rather than when she is embroiled in conflict. Reasoning with children at this or any age requires knowing when to reason — and when simply to take action.

You should also be prepared for the fact that beginning at two or three, your child may readily invent stories that sound like deliberate falsehoods but really are healthy exercises of fantasy — and you should accept them as such. In addition to this type of falsehood, fours often try to cover their tracks, not to deceive you, because they do not yet understand deception, but to avert the consequences of their acts. Your youngster might blame a friend or family member for damage she has done — like one child who, when confronted with the deep scratch across a favorite record, insisted "Daddy did it." Lying at this age and earlier, however, is morally innocent behavior — the child's attempt to make reality conform to the way she wants it to be.

Keep in mind that it is harder for children to understand why lying is wrong than to grasp why a visible action such as hitting

These sociable four-year-olds are modeling their behavior on that of their mothers. While one little girl carefully sets a pretty table, her friend gives a doll a lecture in proper table manners. The child herself may not yet be displaying these manners regularly at the table; she can repeat rules before she learns to follow them consistently.

or stealing is wrong. Your child does not yet understand either the invisible moral quality of trust or the fact that lying is wrong because it destroys trust. But it is now time to begin developing this idea. Let your child know that it makes you happy when she tells the truth, because then you can believe what she says.

Fours like the limelight, and they come up with all sorts of ways to get it. In play with peers, as with adults, your four-year-old will sometimes be bossy, and she may do things wrong on purpose to get a playmate or parent to react. Try to enjoy the antics when you can and spend time just playing with her so you are not always in the role of the authority. Reserve your firmest guidance for such inflexible issues as safety, unreasonable aggression and destruction of property.

Even more than younger children, fours are capable of altruistic actions and attitudes when their desires do not conflict with someone else's. Preschool teachers often note genuine acts of compassion at this age — such as helping a hurt child or keeping one child from pushing another. It is important for parents to nurture these empathic tendencies even as they are dealing with the new wave of testing behaviors.

Five to Six Years

By the age of five, the child shows definite signs of becoming a reliable, stable individual. He has learned to control his behavior to the point where he is not as likely to trammel the rights of others. He is better at sharing. His language ability permits him to understand and absorb more of the lessons his parents seek to teach him. A growing vocabulary, on the other hand, also enables him to use speech aggressively, and he may argue more. Still, this is the age in which he turns into a junior conformist; this makes the youngster easier to handle, since he is motivated by a greater-than-ever need to please and a desire to look and act like others.

The typical five-year-old wants nothing more than to be like the other children he admires, and he gets along with them well. His play behavior is generally cooperative and peaceful, yet he also likes competitive games, which may require adult supervision to preserve order.

The brand-new kindergartner may have secret anxieties about the strange place and routines he is encountering. Believing rules to be absolute, the youngster fears disobeying the teacher's orders, but he has a difficult time assimilating all of them quickly and therefore may need to receive extra attention and reassurance at home for a little while.

As he approaches the age of six, the child makes rapid strides in his ability to distinguish between the intended and the accidental effects of his actions and those of others. He is better able to forgive someone's stepping on his toes if the person says that it was an accident and is sorry. However, he is still not above stealing and lying. In the youngster's mind, the badness he knows these acts represent is outweighed by his need to have a prized object or to tell a story to his own satisfaction.

In the course of his normal development, the five-year-old has absorbed much of his parents' morality system and at times acts on the basis of it. He takes rules more seriously than ever, but has not yet fully internalized them. He has the makings of a conscience now, but he still defines actions as either right or wrong primarily to please his parents and teachers and to avoid punishment, rather than to satisfy some inner standard of conduct. The kindergartner still has a long way to travel on the road to moral maturity, but he has made important progress toward becoming a good, responsible, self-regulating human being — the final goal of all behavior lessons.

Proud to be a helping member of the family, a five-year-old brings the salad to the table during dinner with Grandma and Grandpa. Five-year-olds enjoy making contributions of their own to home life, a way of asserting themselves and also of winning praise.

23

Experiences That Shape a Child

Although all children follow roughly the same developmental path to sociable behavior, each youngster is inevitably influenced by the particular experiences of his growing years. The earliest of these influences are the bonds of dependency, trust and love that form between the new infant and his parents *(pages 8-9)*. But in the months and years to come, even though parents will remain the primary shapers of a child's behavior, their influence will be increasingly augmented by that of other people, among them child-care providers, relatives and the child's own peers.

Moreover, reality is such that children cannot be protected from the unexpected upheavals that can occur in their young lives — including, perhaps, even the breakup of the family. Behavior is often swayed by such events, but the stronger the child's basic emotional ties to his mother and father, the better he is likely to fare.

Parents as models These emotional ties, in fact, provide a child's earliest incentive to behave in a socially acceptable fashion. When a baby feels secure in his parents' love, he develops a natural desire to please them and to win their approval. He soon learns that he can earn these pleasant rewards by repeating behaviors they consider good and avoiding the bad ones — even though he may not yet understand why this is so.

The process of absorbing his parents' values is helped along by the young child's natural tendency to imitate their words and deeds. Children are very keen observers: As he grows from infancy into toddlerhood, your little one takes more and more note of the way you treat him and interact with other people, soaking up your unspoken attitudes as well as the more deliberate lessons you are teaching.

Have no doubt about it: Whenever the two of you are together, your child is learning from you. He takes in how you deal with the clerk at the supermarket, how you cope with losing on the tennis court and what you say about your least favorite politicians when watching the evening news. You cannot afford to be a hypocrite — preaching courtesy, self-control, good sportsmanship, generosity, respect for the law and a dozen other admirable virtues without practicing them yourself.

During a child's preschool years, at least, parents can make the task of teaching good behavior a great deal easier if they curb their all-too-human displays of temper, salty language and disparaging remarks about others in the presence of their child. Children are purists and cannot understand that for every rule there may be an exception. And given how literal-minded they can be, you would do well to avoid telling white lies and stretching the truth, because to your youngster such dodges will seem no different from the falsehoods he is capable of inventing.

Even with the best of intentions, you cannot be perfect around your child all the time. Your child needs to recognize that you, too, must grapple occasionally with feelings of anger, discouragement, selfishness and jealousy, and that sometimes you, too, lose control *(pages 58-59)*. Even if you try to hide your negative side, she will almost certainly notice that something is wrong and, given her egocentric view of the world, may blame herself.

Experts suggest that the best way to handle a bad mood is to tell your child in simple terms that "Mommy is feeling upset just now because someone hollered at her at work," or that "Daddy banged up the car and that makes him angry at himself." Take responsibility for your mood and reassure the youngster that you will get over it soon, and that she does not need to concern herself, except perhaps to give you a hug that makes you feel better. If you do lose your temper or otherwise display less-than-exemplary behavior, you may want to use the lapse as an opportunity to talk about how things can go wrong and what a person can do to make the situation better next time. The most important thing is that you maintain a level of credibility in your youngster's eyes.

Discussing family finances in a calm and agreeable manner, this couple sets an example for cooperative behavior. Their children absorb such lessons and — with Mother's encouragement — are willing to practice cooperation themselves in a dispute over a toy truck.

The marriage relationship

If the parent-child relationship is of primary importance in shaping the child's character, so the parents' marriage can set a standard. Parents who feel comfortable in their marriage and have peaceable ways of resolving conflicts create a favorable atmosphere in which their child can learn trust and cooperation. When parents are sharply critical of each other or have open disagreements about responsibilities, parenting techniques and the behaviors and values they want to instill, they are almost certain to raise a child with an unsure hold on her own values.

Most marriages fall somewhere in between these extremes, with parents trying their best to arrive at a consensus on behavior and discipline but never fully succeeding. If the latter description fits your marriage, you and your spouse should try to show your child a united front even in the midst of disagreement. Later, when you are alone together, you can discuss your differences and seek a common ground.

The effects of a broken marriage

When a marital breakup occurs, parents are often tempted to change their parenting style; many lower their behavioral standards in the belief that a youngster's anger and confusion will diminish if she is allowed to have her way. However, experts insist that just the opposite is the case: The child does not experience such indulgence as an expression of love, but as a form of neglect or abandonment. She craves the consistency and continuity that discipline played in her life before her parents separated. Many children going through the first throes of their parents' divorce demonstrate their need for greater adult control with a variety of testing behaviors ranging from tantrums to stealing, destroying property, hitting and telling lies. Others regress temporarily into infantile dependency, clinging to one or both parents and becoming extremely shy and fearful of others.

Studies of children during and after divorce show that it is not the separation of parents per se that is likely to cause a child to be angry, depressed and unruly, but the open conflict that many divorcing couples display. Interestingly, children who have lost a parent to death are less likely to experience severe behavior problems than those whose parents break up. Divorcing parents should do their best to cooperate with each other; any words or actions that undermine the youngster's affection for either parent can only be destructive to her own sense of self-worth and security. The parents should also reassure the child that although Mom and Dad cannot live together any more, they both will always love her and care about her future.

Stepparenting and discipline

The child who adjusts to having a single parent, or to living alternately with both natural parents, is frequently confronted with a new and more challenging set of problems when one of his parents takes a new partner. Suddenly stepchild and stepparent are tossed together in a relationship in which each has an unfamiliar new title but no real sense of parent-child connection, no sense of the other's temperament, living habits or expectations. The stepparent may be so anxious to be liked that he or she is reluctant to assert authority in the household. The stepchild can be just as anxious to show her loyalty to the absent parent by defying the newcomer altogether.

Experience has shown that stepparents generally fare best in their new families when they take up the reins of discipline cautiously and unaggressively, allowing the natural parent to act as the primary disciplinarian in the first weeks and months of readjustment. Some experts recommend that the newcomer avoid solo confrontations with a youngster until a bridge of friendship and trust has been established. At the same time, the stepparent cannot afford to position himself as a pushover or as someone who will allow the child to play parent against parent. He can be authoritative without being authoritarian. Finally, he must accept the reality that it is seldom possible or even proper to make fundamental changes in the child's developing value system and lifestyle. It is not only the child who will resent the attempt: so will the natural parent, who may feel that her own values are under attack. For better or for worse then, the stepparent is best advised to restrict teaching behavior and discipline to those actions that directly impinge upon daily family life and to leave the rest to others who have known the youngster longer.

Sibling relationships Much has been said and written about the rivalry that is supposedly built into the relationship between siblings, but the fact is that brothers and sisters can interact in many positive ways. With one another as social equals, each child has an opportunity to test a wide range of behavior patterns, from conflict and competition to compassion, loyalty and protectiveness, in the safe confines of the family.

Whereas the firstborn generally has only his parents as models, the younger child is likely to look to an older sibling as a sometime example for either good or bad behavior. Thus, the youngster who is the victim of an older sister's or brother's bullying may reasonably want to inflict similar behavior on a peer, if only for the compensatory reward of feeling powerful himself. By the same token, the youngster who sees his older sibling performing acts of generosity in the family or striving for excellence in school, and being widely praised for it, is likely to adopt similar behaviors. Happily, the older child can also profit from such a relationship, gaining self-esteem in being the object of the younger child's admiration.

A first child almost always greets the arrival of a new baby with behavior changes. Some children become more demanding and selfish; others respond with new-found self-reliance and an eagerness to help with infant care. Part of the difference probably lies in the older child's temperament, but specialists believe that the way parents deal with the changes has an even more significant effect on the outcome. If the older child feels genuinely displaced in terms of parental attention, and all sorts of new responsibilities are thrust upon him with no new privileges to balance them out, then the firstborn will almost certainly resent the baby to one degree or another. But if the parents use the baby's infantile behavior as an opportunity to help the older child feel proud about his new, more grown-up status, the firstborn can continue to feel special in his parents' eyes — and may even delight in helping with the baby's care. Whatever the age of the older child, parents should openly empathize with him, letting him know they understand his feelings.

The extended family Aunts, uncles and grandparents also serve as important behavior-molders in some families. In cases where they see the child for brief periods of time but over many years, relatives are

in the enviable position of forging a loving bond without the specific expectations and goals that complicate parent-child relationships. You need not worry about a grandparent or favorite aunt spoiling a young child with food treats, trips to the toy store and other special indulgences during occasional visits. If you are regularly enforcing your own behavioral standards, such lapses will do no serious harm, and the pleasure and warm feelings they produce may very well help the youngster feel closer ties to Grandpa or Aunt Ellie when they are separated by distance again.

On the other hand, if you have extended family members who live nearby and care for your child on a more-than-occasional basis, a clash between your behavior standards and theirs can create problems. A mother or a sister-in-law may consider her child-rearing policies preferable to yours. Because she has a special interest in your youngster's well-being, she may feel she is actually doing you a favor by following her own instincts when it comes to letting your child talk back or eat candy. Yet many parents are understandably reluctant to challenge a family member who is providing free baby-sitting services.

Should you find yourself facing this dilemma, first try to explain your disciplinary policies to the relative and get her cooperation. If you still cannot reach an understanding, you will have to take a hard look at the situation and decide whether the financial benefits are worth the price you are paying in aggravation to yourself and confusion to your child.

Child-care providers

If you are a working parent and your child spends a better part of his day with a hired caregiver — either in your home or at a child-care center — that person is going to exert considerable influence on your youngster. Your child will undoubtedly need to be disciplined at times in your absence — waiting until Mommy gets home is too late — and careful planning is critical if you expect the youngster to be dealt with as you wish. So make a point of focusing on behavior and discipline issues when you are interviewing prospective caregivers *(page 30)*. Once you have hired someone, work closely with her to make sure your guidelines are being carried out.

You will have the most control over the situation with a caregiver who works in your home. Because this person has a concentrated, one-to-one relationship with your child, it is important that you take the time to describe your policies thoroughly. Outline your house rules and explain how you want your child disciplined when he breaks them. If you deal with hitting by putting your child in a time-out, for instance, show the caregiver how to use the technique *(page 55).* Tell her about any special routines or chores, as well. For example, if your child is expected to pick up his toys before dinner, make this rule clear.

Realistically, you cannot expect to exert as much control when you leave your youngster in a group-care situation, either in someone else's home or in a center. But always do as much as you can to get your caregiver aligned with your own discipline approaches. And whatever your child-care situation, you will want to ask the caregiver about her day with your child. What activities did he seem to enjoy or dislike? Were there any special behavior problems? How did the caregiver handle them? Do not feel as though you are prying; you have the right and responsibility to make sure your child is being cared for as you wish.

Finally, when you are not satisfied with the way things are going, and attempts to work out the problem have failed, the wisest course is simply to find someone else to care for your child; you have better things to do with your time and energy than spend them righting behavioral wrongs that a child-care provider has thoughtlessly encouraged.

Discipline and the working parent

The child-care issue aside, growing up in a family with two working parents can, in itself, have a significant effect on a child's behavior. Such mothers and fathers are forced to squeeze their

Matching Discipline and Day Care

For working couples, choosing a caregiver or day-care center whose style of discipline reflects their own is a matter of paramount importance. The following tips should aid the selection process.

The caregiver who comes to your home:
Look for a person with a positive, constructive view of life, someone who is likely to reinforce your child's positive behavior, rather than harp on the negative. Watch her interact with your child. Does she appear to be someone who enjoys small children and who will be actively involved with the youngsters in her care?

Find out how she disciplines. Begin by asking her directly about her methods: Does she use corporal punishment of any kind? Does she have the stamina to wait out a tantrum and the patience to teach a child self-help skills?

You might also give her specific situations — your child's sudden refusal to take his nap, for example, or to eat lunch — and invite her to describe to you how she would handle such situations. And last,

when you call the caregiver's references, be sure to find out how she disciplined their children.

Determine the prospective caregiver's willingness to follow the routine you have worked out for your youngster. Will her own schedule give her time to discuss with you any discipline problems requiring your attention?

The caregiver who works in her home:
In addition to pursuing the pointers above, you should take a look around the caregiver's home environment. Is it conducive to good behavior? Or does it contain temptations that are likely to get children into trouble, such as easily reached stereo equipment, delicate knickknacks and potted plants?

If there are other children in her charge, see how the caregiver handles them and how they play together. Does the caregiver seem inclined to park the children in front of the television as a way of curbing their activity and controlling their behavior?

The day-care center:
Find out what experience the center's teachers and aides have. Do they know what kind of behavior to expect of children your youngster's age?

What is the staff turnover rate? Look for a center that has a stable staff: Teachers need to work with your child on an ongoing basis in order to deal effectively with behavioral problems.

Get permission to observe the children and staff interacting. How do the teachers handle youngsters when they refuse to comply with directions, or when they behave aggressively, for example? How often do the teachers praise the youngsters for their achievements? Do the children seem happy and busy, or excessively controlled? Will the center allow you to make an occasional unannounced visit?

Find out whether the center encourages regularly scheduled teacher-parent conferences, and if the teacher is available at the end of the day to discuss behavior issues. If necessary, can you call and discuss your concerns by phone?

parenting efforts into the relatively few waking hours they share with their offspring each day. Many feel guilty about spending so much prime time away from their child in the first place, and as a result, they are tempted to waive discipline altogether.

To be sure, it takes a special effort to deal with behavior issues after a long workday, when all parties are tired and a bit cranky, and the demands of dinner, bath and bedtime are pressing. Experts insist, however, that it is every bit as important to establish and enforce routines and rules in a two-career household as it is in one where a parent is home with the children all day. Whatever the family's daily schedule involves, a child needs to have guidelines and limits set on her behavior, so that she will be able to develop her own internal controls — the ultimate goal of all lessons in good behavior.

Peer relationships
As children grow older, they become more and more involved in play with other children and increasingly look to them as models for behavior *(pages 94-95)*. Peers typically help socialize each other by reinforcing a wide range of positive actions and attitudes, from cooperation and generosity to sharing and helping. Young children are quick to perceive that those who shine in these areas generally attract more friends than those who are selfish and aggressive. The shy or timid youngster may also become more sociable through repeated exposure to a more outgoing playmate.

Two well-matched playmates discover the joys of having a close buddy. By the age of five peers begin to exercise greater influence on one another, providing support, example and the opportunity to experiment with new behaviors.

Just as important, from about your child's third birthday onward, peer relationships offer her an opportunity to deal with other people as equals, rather than as the older, larger and wiser authority figures who have dominated her life to this point. Unlike her relationships with her mother and father and other adults, social liaisons with other boys and girls are largely voluntary; the child who feels uncomfortable with one playmate has the option to find another companion who is better suited to her temperament.

This new ability to choose friends is an important developmental leap for a preschooler. It enables her to broaden her social contacts, to experiment with a variety of behaviors and to practice her fledgling decision-making powers. As she grows out of the early childhood years and into school age, the ability to map out her own social path will open the door to a vast new world of independent, self-directed behavior. ❖

The Fine Art of Discipline

Many mothers and fathers associate the word "discipline" with punishment and see it as their duty to correct their children's behavior through a variety of stern measures, including spanking. Yet punishing a child is only one small part of discipline, and corrections can be made without harshness, as in the photograph opposite, where a mother is telling her daughter face to face what she does not like about her behavior and how the little girl can improve it. In fact, true discipline is a caring process and a creative one as well, which should bring out the best in a child.

Unqualified love and reasonable limits are the twin components of all effective discipline. Using both, parents can guide their children toward good behavior. Once you have discovered all the positive methods of discipline that are available to you, you can reserve punishment as a very last resort. Even then you will find that you can carry it out without humiliating your youngster, yet still teach her a lesson.

Discipline requires that you establish a balanced system of rules and that you enforce them consistently so that your child will always know where you and she both stand. Discipline also requires the kind of home atmosphere and environment that promotes good behavior. Inevitably, however, there will be occasional setbacks. You must be ready for them and able to get a grip on your anger at your misbehaving child.

Discipline, then, is an art that takes time to learn and to practice. And your skills will improve dramatically with use. The occasional mistakes you make will fade quickly from your youngster's memory if you express your love for her openly, respect her unique needs and shape your expectations accordingly.

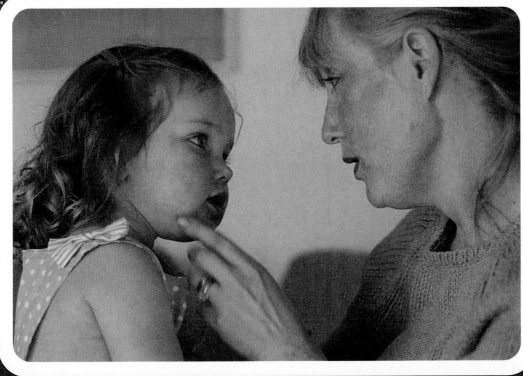

Playing by the Rules

Good disciplining requires not just love and patience, but clarity of purpose. Nothing works better than a reasonable set of rules that establish boundaries beyond which the child may not stray without encountering parental intervention. From the outset, both parents should agree on the standards they wish to lay down and understand their reasons for applying them. In devising rules for very young children, however, parents must assess the child's readiness to learn and follow behavioral guidelines *(pages 18-23)*. A long list of do's and don'ts is beyond the ability of the average two-year-old to obey, let alone comprehend.

Setting priorities

The first rules you make, in the early years when a child is not mature enough to understand the potential consequences of her actions, should be designed to ensure her safety. That knife glistening on the kitchen counter, for example, attracts her attention because of its sparkle. She has no inkling that its sharp edge could cut her. She must rely on her parents to set the limit here.

As the child matures, rules can grow in number and variety, but by no means should they become so numerous that they overwhelm and confuse. You, as a parent, will want to set priorities and to take into account your needs, along with your youngster's, when devising principles of behavior for her to follow.

Effective discipline also requires time, patience and above all a willingness to teach — rather than merely impose — the rules you have laid down. You must be able to explain them as often as may be required to get them across.

The benefit of limits

By setting limits on your child's behavior, being consistent in their application and spelling out the consequences that her actions can lead to, you are adding to her sense of security. She knows what to expect of you and of herself. As she increasingly internalizes what you have taught her, she gains in self-control, self-respect and independence; she will incorporate your values, as well as your rules, and thus be able to make more and more effective decisions on her own concerning her behavior. The ultimate goal of imposing and enforcing rules is, after all, to teach the child how to regulate her own actions. Once you have worked out a system of equable and realistic rules, try to keep the following principles in mind as you apply them:

Discipline constructively. Use simple words and a voice that is authoritative but not bossy. Situation permitting, say "Please do this," more often than "Don't do that!" And be flexible. For example, if you see that your child is tired, you might put off asking him to put his blocks away until after he has had his nap.

Discipline consistently. Do not let the child get away with a behavioral no-no one time and then come down hard on him the next time. This will befuddle him and weaken your authority.

Tell why rules must be followed. Instead of issuing a terse "because I told you so," explain the rationale behind your decisions and rules. But be sure to make it brief; long explanations usually leave a youngster distracted. With the reasons explained, the child is in a better position not only to obey, but to absorb the behavior and make it his own.

Never demean or embarrass your child. Discipline is not meant to shame or embarrass. Always treat your youngster gently and, whenever possible, discipline him in private. From time to time, put yourself in his shoes and remember those times when as a child you were disciplined and how you felt about it.

Discipline honestly. If you have a sound, realistic reason for wanting your child to adhere to your standard, and can explain it to him, that is enough. Do not cajole him or attempt to make him feel guilty for an act in the hope that you can play on his guilt the next time he misbehaves. Children dislike being manipulated as much as adults do, and it will make them just as angry.

Discipline without comparisons. It will get you nowhere to point out to a youngster whom you are chastising how much better a sibling or a playmate behaves. He can learn from the example of others, but not when under pressure. Comparisons at such moments are only likely to encourage his defiance.

Discipline at the moment. Do not delay the consequences of your child's misbehavior. The old dodge "Just wait till Daddy comes home!" is not an effective way to deal with behavior problems. Postponing punishment creates undue anxiety in the child, and the impact of the discipline is diluted when the punishment is distanced from the act.

Monitor the results of your discipline efforts. Whatever techniques you choose to use with your child, always observe his reactions closely to make sure your methods are bringing the intended results. If not, modify them or try a new tack.

Do not dwell on issues. There is a great deal of truth in the familiar refrain, "This hurts me more than it hurts you." Young children, amazingly resilient, can usually absorb discipline, adjust and move on while their parents are still fretting over the incident. Once you have taken action, let the matter be over.

Offer praise and encouragement when your child responds positively to your discipline. Nothing works as well as approval, and your child will be eager to show you how he can follow rules once he has obtained your blessing. ⋰

Setting the Stage for Good Behavior

Children do not learn behavior in a vacuum any more than they grow up in one. They and the way they act are the product of many forces, inside and outside the home, and parents who recognize this have an advantage when it comes to teaching effective behavior. The exasperated mother who laments that "I just can't do a thing with Johnny" has failed to see that his misconduct may have as much to do with the circumstances surrounding each episode as the situation that provoked it. Indeed, she may be one of the reasons why he is misbehaving.

Typically, such a mother complains about Johnny's constant refusal to cooperate without understanding how she herself is opening the door to noncooperation. "Getting him to put on his coat is such a chore," she says. But what does she do each time? She gives him a command disguised as a question: "Do you want to put on your coat now?" Of course, Johnny does not want to put it on — certainly not when he is in the middle of play. But the

Play has gotten out of hand here, but once the host parents realized that it was not the children who were at fault, but themselves for inviting too many guests, they knew what to do next time. In the illustration opposite, their daughter plays happily the following afternoon with just one friend.

mother who is prepared, who stands ready with coat in hand, takes her son by the arm and says firmly, "Now, Matt, we're going to put on your coat," achieves the results she wants. Having anticipated Matt's possible resistance, she has avoided it and thus is in charge of the situation. In the case of the questioning mother, it is Johnny who is in charge.

The important thing is to recognize that, to a large extent, behavior can be controlled, and pitfalls avoided by foresight. This means creating the kind of loving atmosphere in which good behavior can flourish. Among other things, it entails a home environment free of temptations that could get your child into trouble, a well thought-out routine that will keep him on an even keel and the kind of clear, warm communication that will let him know where he stands and what is expected of him.

Factors that affect behavior

Learning how to behave well is basically a matter of conditioning. When a youngster's positive behavior is consistently recognized, it proliferates; when it is ignored, it dwindles and disappears. Your child wants your attention. If he cannot win it by pleasing you, he may go out of his way to irritate you and get it that way. Ironically, many parents pay far more heed to their children when they misbehave than when they are being cooperative. But parents who use a system of incentives based on praise and rewards spend far less time punishing their offspring and more of their energy encouraging good behavior. When your youngster receives your acclaim for closing the door behind him, you can almost be certain that he will close it the next time in anticipation of your favorable response. But if you overlook his act, he is more likely to forget and leave the door open. Your goal should be to reinforce your youngster's positive behavior as often as necessary so that it becomes ingrained.

A way to change behavior

Even when your child's behavior leaves a great deal to be desired, you can do something about it. Experts recommend taking a thoughtful, methodical approach that begins with a precise definition of the offensive behavior. If, for instance, your youngster is impolite, it is not enough to state that she is rude. How is she rude? Does she fail to say please and thank you, or to greet guests properly? Does she jump up from the dinner table and run off without excusing herself? Once you have focused on the problem and defined it, you can begin taking steps to solve it. But in the process you may discover that there are several problems that need working on, all of them linked. If this is the case, choose one problem to address first. Chances are that when you solve it the others will go away.

With the problem defined, you are in a position to analyze it. Look at the antecedents and consequences of the behavior. You may find it useful to jot down your observations. Is there a pattern? Does the problem assert itself at a particular time of day? Is it most prevalent after your child has been with her friends? What part do you and the rest of the family play? If the problem is rudeness, ask yourself whether you are as cognizant of your own manners as you are of hers? Do you, in fact, say please and thank you when you ask her to do something for you? Have you been nagging your youngster to be polite? Does your scolding seem to perpetuate her rudeness rather than eliminate it?

Having observed your child's behavior, the circumstances leading up to it and the way you or others react to it, you will better understand why she behaves the way she does and will

Actions Leading Up to the Misbehavior

Rises at seven each morning.

Eats breakfast.

Watches TV while mother works in kitchen.

Step 1: The Problem

Child is stubborn.

Step 2: Observing the Specific Behaviors

Will not put away the toys in his room.

Balks over going to bed.

In morning, dawdles when asked to get dressed.

Solving a Problem Step by Step

The parents of a five-year-old boy were exasperated by his seeming stubbornness and wanted to do something about it. First they pinpointed examples of his stubbornness. While several behaviors stood out as problems, they picked the situation they wanted to work on right away: his reluctance to dress himself in the morning. Next, they examined the events leading up to his recalcitrance and those that followed. They discovered that the mother was actually reinforcing the very behavior they wanted to eliminate. Finally, by changing the way she responded to the situation, as well as the situation itself, they were able to channel their son's actions in a positive direction. To guarantee success, the boy's parents adhered to the plan until the new behavior was firmly established. The path the family followed is traced in the diagram above.

now be ready for the last step — planning a program to bring about the changes you want. Do not be surprised, however, if you learn that your own behavior as well as your child's requires modification. You may need to set a better example, scold less and praise more.

The diagnostic diagram below follows this method from beginning to end and can serve as a basic model for confronting behavior problems you wish to solve. Since change generally does not occur overnight, you will probably have to repeat some of the steps several times to ensure success, being careful to offer generous praise with each positive advance that your youngster makes.

Your child wants nothing more than to experience success — and success teaches. By prearranging conditions that will lead to good behavior, you will be able to provide him with the positive reinforcement that is the best teacher of all. Start by examining your child's environment to determine whether there is anything in it that is causing him to misbehave, then make the necessary changes. If, for example, your two-year-old frequently

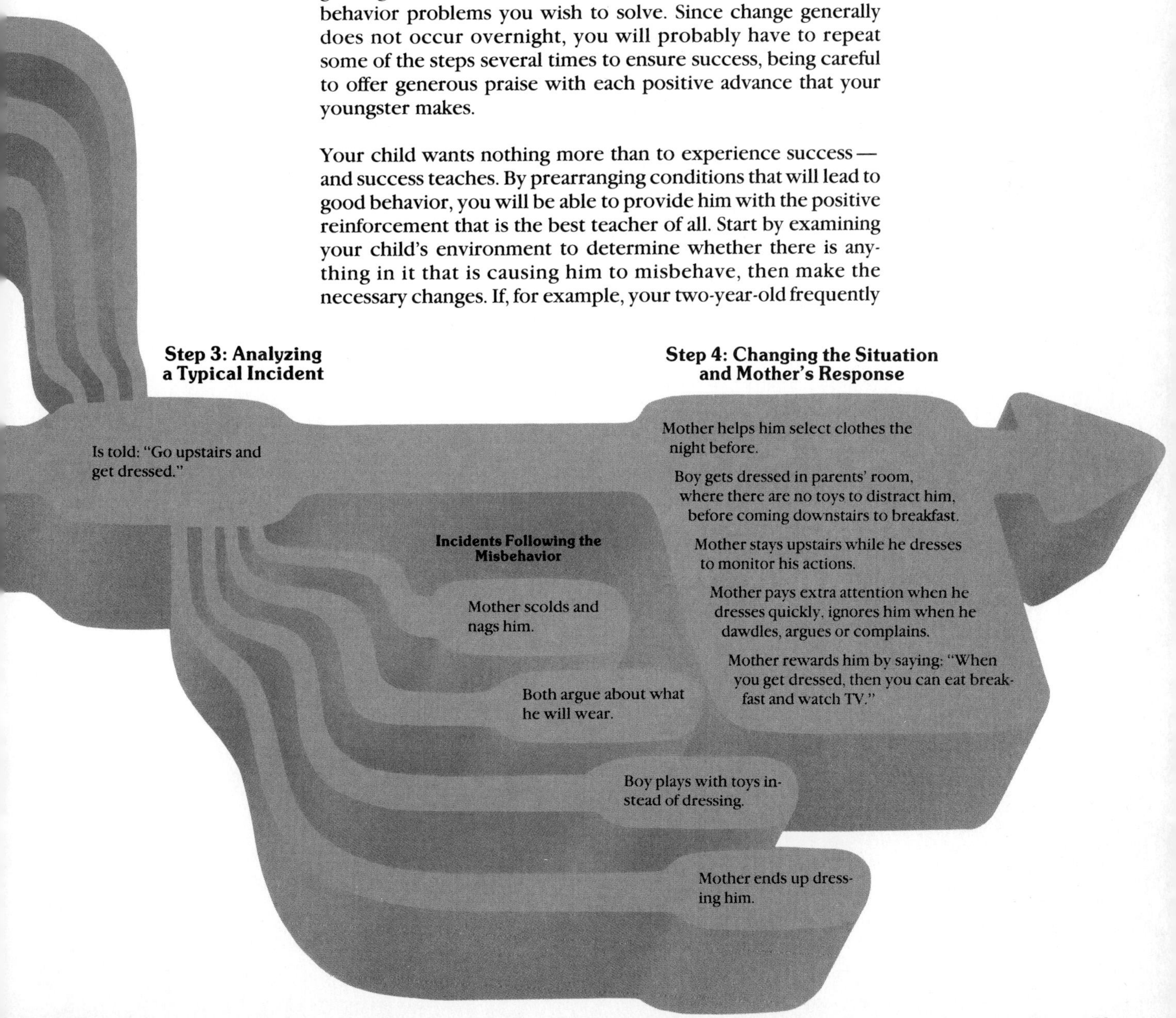

**Step 3: Analyzing
a Typical Incident**

Is told: "Go upstairs and get dressed."

Incidents Following the Misbehavior

Mother scolds and nags him.

Both argue about what he will wear.

Boy plays with toys instead of dressing.

Mother ends up dressing him.

**Step 4: Changing the Situation
and Mother's Response**

Mother helps him select clothes the night before.

Boy gets dressed in parents' room, where there are no toys to distract him, before coming downstairs to breakfast.

Mother stays upstairs while he dresses to monitor his actions.

Mother pays extra attention when he dresses quickly, ignores him when he dawdles, argues or complains.

Mother rewards him by saying: "When you get dressed, then you can eat breakfast and watch TV."

flicks on your portable radio, punishing him for doing so is merely a temporary solution that teaches very little. In fact, he will probably try again when you are not looking. By focusing on the real problem — leaving the radio where he can reach it — you can solve it. Remove the radio from his reach on the table and place it on a shelf. You can then use the radio to satisfy his curiosity and to teach a lesson. Tell your youngster he can turn it on for a special program each day, under your supervision, and take the opportunity to show him how the various buttons and knobs work.

Again, with a little forethought you can keep your child out of mischief by creating the kind of busy atmosphere in which good behavior grows. Fill his day with constructive activities of many different kinds, planning them carefully and perhaps even drawing up a handy list that you can refer to. There will be a big benefit to you in this: You will be relieved of some of the frustration that can grow out of your wish to get on with your work and your need to divert your child. You will want him within view, of course, so place his books or toys where you can keep an eye on him. When cooking, you might let him have some bowls or spoons to play with or give him a cardboard box that can be his pretend stove.

Children love having things to do as much as adults, but since they have shorter attention spans, it is always a good idea to suggest a switch to something new whenever you see your youngster starting to grow restless. You can use different activities to distract him at critical moments. Bringing out his books when he is tired of playing with his blocks may be just the diversion the child needs in order to keep his boredom from turning into mischief.

With a toddler, distraction can be used to particular advantage. Children at this age are not purposefully naughty, but like the little boy with the radio, they are naturally curious. If your child insists on taking books down from the shelf, pick him up and call his attention to the bird on the window sill, then present him with his trucks or a puzzle. If he loves to play with the television remote control, do not just remove it from his hands; give him a suitable replacement, such as a toy calculator with plenty of buttons to push.

This mother has made playing with the TV a no-no. But rather than scolding her son for doing so, she stands ready with a toy to divert his attention and engage him in a more constructive activity.

The need for routine

Children are creatures of habit. With all the uncertainties and frustrations your child faces each day as his world grows ever bigger, he needs a routine that will give him a sense of order and security. By working out a reasonable schedule for meals, playtime, naps and other activities, you will not only be promoting his physical well-being, but providing him with the stability essential to good behavior. The child who has a regular routine is less likely to be cranky — and thus will be a lot more cooperative than one whose days are disordered and unstructured.

Once you have established a daily routine for your youngster, follow it consistently. This does not mean that you should adhere to it as though it were an inflexible timetable. No child likes being yanked from one activity to another. You may wish to prolong the game or task that has engaged your youngster's attention before having him move on to something else. You can always get him used to the idea with a five-minute warning: "In five minutes we will put the game away and get ready for naptime." That will help avoid an unnecessary confrontation.

Avoiding misbehavior away from home

When you and your child visit your friends or relatives, or you travel some distance from home, a little advance preparation on your part will encourage good behavior. Your youngster may well be uneasy over the prospect of the unfamiliar, not knowing what lies in store or how she should behave. Have her bring along her doll or a few favorite playthings, packed perhaps in her own little bag. Tell her what to expect and explain to her how she might feel and react. Always focus on the positive. For instance, if you are going to pay a call on a great-aunt, you might say something like this to your youngster a couple of hours before leaving: "We're going to visit Great-Aunt Miriam. She will be happy to see you. She is not able to hear very well, so she may ask you to speak up. She likes to play the piano. Maybe she will let you play, too."

Allow choices

Permit your child some choice in activities. Choosing helps her hone her decision-making skills and encourages independence as well as good behavior. It will also tell you something about her evolving competence and changing needs and show you how to adjust her schedule to take these into account. When offering choices, however, make sure you present real options, especially since these determine behavior. "You can either play outside without throwing sand at your sister, or you can come inside and play in your room alone" is the kind of clear statement that offers the child a chance to decide for herself what behavior to adopt.

Ready for a trip, a little boy has his own binoculars and a knapsack filled with toys. His mother knows that thus equipped he will not grow restless as the journey progresses, and that the youngster will be easier to handle than if bored.

41

The importance of explaining why

Children, of course, model much of their behavior on that of their parents, but they learn not just by example; they need to know why parents approve of some kinds of behavior and not of others. Be prepared to tell your child the reasons for your actions as often as you can so that he will understand why he should adopt your values and emulate your behavior. He may wonder why you buy groceries for the old woman down the street; tell him that the woman lives alone and is too frail to go out on her own and that you like helping her. Point out to your youngster that some behaviors are appropriate in one situation and inappropriate in another. Talking out loud may be all right on the street, but it is not all right in a house of worship when people are praying. And make sure that what you teach and how you act are in fact consonant — otherwise, you will leave your child confused.

Communicating well

Good communication promotes good behavior for the simple reason that the child who knows what your expectations for her are can more easily live up to them. Discussions are a fine way to get your message across and hear your child out as well. When talking to her, come down to her level verbally and, as often as possible, physically too. Kneel or crouch and use words appropriate to her age, spoken clearly in a gentle voice. Make certain that she has grasped what you have said — and that you have understood her, too. Never lecture, preach or ridicule.

To help your child learn how to converse, avoid asking her yes-or-no questions; ask, instead, for her opinions and then accept them nonjudgmentally. You may have to bite your lip to keep from laughing at her replies, but in doing so you are showing her that you take her seriously.

About to drop a ball on his playmates' construction, this youngster needs a reprimand. But instead of talking to him in the presence of his friends, his mother wisely takes him aside (opposite) and disciplines him in private, preventing him from being embarrassed by her intervention.

You may want to follow the example of some parents who establish a special daily attention time, during which they give their child a chance to talk things over with them. This is especially useful when both parents work. A regularly scheduled family meeting can also be of benefit, with each member allowed time to voice his or her feelings and opinions. This works best with older children. A two- or three-year-old can participate in such family conferences, but her short attention span will prevent her from getting much out of them if the sessions exceed 10 to 15 minutes.

The importance of listening

By no means is communication all a matter of words. It involves such body language as smiles, hugs and kisses — and it means listening. When you listen carefully to your youngster and project empathy and respect, you demonstrate your trust and your confidence in him. You are letting him know that he is entitled to his own perceptions and beliefs — even when they do not match yours. This critical lesson will serve him well when he steps out into the world and has to communicate with others.

How to listen

When your child seems eager to tell you something, give her your full attention. Fold up your newspaper, shut off the TV or set aside whatever else you are doing. Turn toward her and look her in the eye. Offer her all the encouragement you can without interrupting her. When she is finished, you might restate what she said in slightly different words to demonstrate that you have heard and understood her, or you might ask a simple question such as, "How do you feel about that?" But you should be careful not to pressure the child.

Listening as your youngster joyfully expresses positive feelings can be a wonderful experience for both of you. Make her happiness an occasion for mutual rejoicing. When she brings up negative feelings, you will need finesse, especially if you find yourself tempted to moralize or, worse, to deny what she is telling you. Some mothers and fathers become anxious in such situations and make the mistake of trying to tell their child what they think she is experiencing, rather than allowing her to decide for herself.

Name That Feeling

When you discuss your child's feelings with her, use words that describe her emotions best. They will help her to articulate her feelings in the future.

Words for Negative Feelings:

afraid
angry
bored
confused
disappointed
embarrassed
hurt
left out
lonesome
sad
tired
worried

Words for Good Feelings:

confident
eager
excited
happy
loved
pleased
proud
relaxed
relieved
satisfied

Your child may need your help in expressing her feelings. Formulating her point of view when it is hard for her to speak may visibly relax her. Other times, just uttering "Oh" — providing it is said in a caring way — gives her a boost. From time to time, you may find it useful to sum up the situation and suggest a possible solution: "It sounds as though Diana made you very angry today when she insisted on being the mom in the dress-up corner. Maybe tomorrow she will let you be the mom if you let her be the grandma."

If your youngster is too upset or frustrated to express herself at all, allow her some time to collect herself. You yourself may need the time to formulate your own thoughts. If she is very angry, the cooling-off period will be of benefit to both of you. Addressing the issue head on all too often jams up the child's feelings and reinforces the negative. When you find that she is ready to talk, you can help her get a grip on the situation, perhaps by making an educated guess about what is on her mind. If you are wrong, she can correct you. Or, when you understand the problem, you can ask how she might handle it differently another time. Children need to know how to deal constructively with their anger, rather than merely venting it.

Identifying emotions

Helping your child express himself may require practice. While he is speaking, take note of his nonverbal cues as well as his actual words. Ask yourself, "What is he feeling?" and think of a specific word to describe his emotion. Then put that word into a sentence: "Wow, you sound upset," or "You seem bored with school." Pinpointing a feeling by giving it a name will show him how to articulate precisely *(box, right)*. Keep your statements tentative, however; you cannot crawl into your youngster's heart and mind, and feel and think for him.

The child who hears his emotion identified derives great comfort from knowing that you recognize it and that you understand him. In teaching him the words for feelings, you are giving him a vocabulary he can use effectively in the future. Once he can name and share his negative feelings, he is less likely to be burdened by them and will be in a better position to control them.

Providing clear instructions

Part of your everyday communication with your child involves giving her instructions to follow for her own good or for that of others. There is a knack to doing this well. When issuing a command, move close to her, say her name and seek eye contact. Then firmly give your order, adding whatever supporting gestures may be necessary. Tell her exactly what you expect: The precise "Jan, please pick your clothes up off the floor" works much better than the vague "Clean up." Commands should be stated positively whenever possible: Say "Stay on the sidewalk" rather than "Don't go into the street." And be sure to give one command at a time; a child will only be confused by a series of them, not knowing which to obey first.

Pause and think before issuing a command you might regret later or have to back down from. If you must retreat, tell your youngster that you changed your mind; this is better than leaving a threat hanging over her.

Make your commands reasonable. Stopping to take your child's age into account, you may realize that she is not ready developmentally to respond. It is useless to tell a two-year-old to share her toys when she has no concept of sharing, but you can talk to her about taking turns.

Commands should never be disguised as questions. "Would you like to go to bed?" invites an honest "no." "It's time to go to bed" reflects a reality the child cannot easily argue with, especially if she has gotten used to a routine. Avoid starting a command with "let's" unless you really mean it. Too often parents use this trick to lure their child into compliance when in fact they have no intention of joining or helping her. Also avoid using threatening or verbally abusive, retaliatory or vengeful commands. They will merely create guilt and induce fearful submission. They do nothing to teach good behavior.

It is essential to give a command only once. You do not want your child to get in the habit of thinking you will repeat orders until she complies, or that she need listen only when you have reached the boiling point. If you specify that your command should be carried out right away, allow her five to 10 seconds to begin responding. Then start applauding her for cooperating. If she balks, respond firmly: "Okay, time-out: You will have to sit in your chair until you are ready to cooperate with me." ❖

This mother knows that nonverbal communication is every bit as important as words when teaching good behavior. With a simple gesture she helps her toddler understand that he must put on his slippers right away.

The Value of Praise and Encouragement

Children thrive on the attention of adults. Very little pleases them more than to have their mothers and fathers show interest in what they are doing. Wise parents take advantage of this and praise their girls' and boys' positive actions as often as possible. Thus they reinforce the youngsters' good behavior and encourage them to repeat it. An occasional spontaneous remark, such as, "I like the way you and Sara are working together to build the block city," teaches good behavior and fosters self-esteem.

Reinforcing good behavior takes time and effort on the part of parents. It is not always easy for young children to learn new social skills. Why should they want to share their toys or interrupt their play to come greet Daddy's friend? But if each stride forward is consistently noticed, commended and rewarded, they will be increasingly motivated to adopt the new behavior.

Showing approval

Recognition can take numerous forms — everything from a few well-chosen words of praise, an embrace, a thumbs-up sign or a wink, to some more tangible reward, such as the bestowal of a privilege or a special treat. But every bit as important to reinforcement is the speed with which approval is shown: The praise should be immediate, so that the child can make the connection between her act and the pleasant consequences that follow.

The knack of praising

It takes skill to praise well. The trick is to praise particular behavior rather than make general comments and to praise often. "What a good girl you are!" is not nearly so effective a reinforcer as a specific: "You've been very patient to play quietly while I've been making dinner." Such a statement tells the child exactly

what you liked about her behavior, as well as what she can do next time to earn similar praise from you.

Keep compliments simple and honest. Like adults, children are put off by gushy or condescending statements. And they are apt to shrink at praise that comes with criticism or reminders of past failures. "Well, it's about time you did it!" is faint praise indeed. How much better to say: "I'm so glad you put your socks in the drawer. I knew you could keep up the good work!"

When your youngster is engaged in a difficult or prolonged activity, do not wait until she has completed it to applaud her accomplishment. Instead, offer encouragement along the way. "That's hard to do and you're doing just fine" is the kind of supportive remark a child loves to hear.

When reinforcing behavior, never hurry the child and never expect change right away. If your goal is to get your youngster to sit still for 20 minutes each night at the dinner table, you should praise her attempts in this direction throughout the meal — every couple of minutes in the case of a toddler, less often with an older youngster. And you must be willing to do so for several nights running until your child successfully adopts the behavior. This sounds like work, and it is — but it will not be in vain. The outcome of reinforcement is not only a more cooperative youngster, but a better parent-child relationship, in which the parent winds up spending less time hassling over daily routines.

The value of tangible rewards

Accompanying praise with an occasional something extra can help establish good behavior. The reward need not be anything elaborate, so long as it is one the child likes, such as a park outing

A father teaches his son to bag leaves, but he knows that a child this young needs constant encouragement. By praising the boy's every effort, he builds confidence.

or an invitation to a friend to come over. Often a statement as simple as "after you brush your teeth, you can watch TV for 10 minutes" works — here it speeds up a dawdling child. But if behavior is to become habit, praise and reward must be repeated as often as necessary until the behavior is learned. Sometimes children have relapses, in which case parents should resume using incentives to bring about the desired behavior.

One effective way to reinforce good behavior is to sit down with your child and list on separate pieces of paper the various privileges or treats she would like to earn for her compliance. Then drop the slips into a jar. When she has displayed the desired behavior, invite her to dip into the jar and take out a slip. Praising her, bestow the reward. You will have a happy and excited child, full of self-confidence — who will be eager to please you again. Another relatively painless but effective way to change your youngster's behavior is to record her efforts on a wall chart so that she can follow her day-by-day progress *(box, opposite).* Then when she has reached the goal you have set for her, you can reward her for her achievement.

Although children should always be permitted to help choose their rewards, they should never be allowed to demand rewards for what they deem to be their accomplishments. Let your youngster know that parents are the ones who dispense rewards and only they can decide when these are to be granted.

The difference between a reward and a bribe

Some parents confuse rewards with bribes. A reward is promised before a child is asked to do something, as a way of eliciting a positive response and reinforcing good behavior. Not least of its virtues is that it leaves the parent in control. A bribe is offered after a youngster has refused to comply with a request, as a means of inducing him to do so. In a typical bribe situation, a mother who has asked her child, say, to clean up the mess he has made playing with clay, reacts to his obstinancy with: "If you clean up the clay, I'll take you to the park." Now the child is in control, free still to refuse, and he has been taught a bad lesson — that through noncompliance he can get what he wants. A wiser mother would have corrected the youngster right away, saying firmly, "Okay, time-out for not listening," and enforced the punishment until the child cleaned up the mess.

The ultimate outcome To keep tangible rewards from losing their efficacy, dispense them judiciously and gradually reduce them as the behavior catches on. Fortunately, praise alone will often suffice to bring about compliance. The child whose good behavior has been reinforced mostly with praise will learn to internalize the good feeling it engenders and be able later to pat himself on the back, rather than needing approval from others. ❖

Reaping Rewards for Star Behavior

One easy way to motivate children to improve their behavior is to record their positive strides on a chart hung in a conspicuous place for all to see. The chart should be as simple as possible. Divide it up by the days of the week and list one or two specific behaviors you wish changed. Every time your youngster shows improvement, make a notation on the chart, using a symbol of his choosing, such as a star or a funny face. Commend the child whenever you make an entry and encourage others in the family to do so too. If the youngster's behavior does not live up to expectations, just leave the space empty and tell

him that you hope he will remember to do better tomorrow.

Seeing the blanks fill up can be reward enough for your three-year-old, but your older child will need the reinforcement of a daily or weekly reward, which you both have settled on in advance, such as an extra story at bedtime.

Once he has successfully modified his behavior, take down the chart and, if you and he agree, hang a new one so that he can work on another area that needs improving. But you should be sure to reinforce your youngster's changed behavior by continuing to single it out for praise.

Jesse's Week

Jesse's Daily Jobs	Mon	Tues	Wed	Thurs	Fri	Sat	Sun
Carry dishes to sink after breakfast	⭐	⭐		⭐	⭐		
Pick up toys before dinner		⭐			⭐		⭐

Daily Rewards:

1 ⭐: Extra story before bed
Frozen fruit bar for dessert
Bubble bath

2 ⭐: Board game with Mom or Dad
Extra ½ hour of afternoon t.v.
Play a game of cards with Mom

Weekly Rewards:

12 ⭐: Trip to park with Dad
movie from video store
Dinner from Hamburger Heaven

When Punishment Becomes Necessary

No matter how much you may encourage your child's good behavior, there will be times when her priorities run headlong into yours or when she defiantly insists on testing the limits that you have established for her. You may then have no recourse but to punish her. Just how you do can make all the difference to the child's self-esteem and future behavior, and ultimately to her image of you.

Punishment involves the use of unpleasant consequences to correct a youngster's misbehavior; it is intended to instruct, not to harm or demean. Yet many parents use old-fashioned methods that have a negative rather than a positive effect on their children and can actually damage them. Too often parents think that what worked for them when they were growing up will be good for their offspring, thus repeating the mistakes of the past.

Child specialists disapprove of punishments that are unreasonably harsh and that inflict physical and emotional anguish. The occasional swat on the bottom or rap on the hand is not likely to cause resentment, and they are often used by parents who want to teach an immediate lesson, especially where the child's safety is concerned. But rapping the knuckles with a ruler, a brusque slap in the face or frequent hard spankings can spawn as much negative behavior over the long run as each form of punishment is supposed to remedy *(box, opposite)*. And such spankings can break a child's spirit. Even constant scolding and nagging can be viewed as an assault on a youngster's sensibilities.

No child, any more than any grownup, appreciates being humiliated, and there is no reason why a youngster should undergo a beating or a tongue-lashing, especially when so many more constructive methods for teaching good behavior exist. Repeated harsh punishment leaves some children with the notion that nasty or violent treatment of others is in the end an acceptable way to act. Some children withdraw into themselves when treated this way, while others respond defiantly, repeating the punished behavior as a way of fulfilling a need for attention.

Effective punishment

Children must learn to take responsibility for their behavior. If they break the rules parents have laid down for them after having had these rules carefully explained, then they must be held accountable for their actions. Sometimes just wearing a stern expression or issuing one firm reminder, such as "I asked you to put your pencils away — now please do it," will produce results without any further ado. On occasion, it may even pay to take a philosophical stance and overlook your young one's misbehavior as something that will pass, concentrating your energies on

To Spank or Not to Spank?

How often have you heard another adult say, usually about someone else's youngster, "What that child needs is a good spanking"? The response is common enough to suggest that a great many Americans still see spanking as the way to correct misbehavior. This is understandable. We learn parenting practices from our mothers and fathers, and since most of us were spanked when we were children, it seems the natural thing to do. There is no denying that spanking is quick and convenient, and many who resort to it claim that it works and that it lets the child know who is boss. But is spanking the best approach to discipline? One father who used spanking as a punishment told me that he always felt guilty afterward. "I feel somehow that I've failed, that spanking is wrong, and that it's ridiculous for a grown man to hit a four-year-old," he said.

I agree. I believe that all children need firm, consistent discipline, but I see no need to spank children to enforce it. I am against spanking for many reasons.

Spanking is an abuse of power. If you were to spank a neighbor's child for a serious misdeed, you could be prosecuted for assault. And when you spank your own child, are you not taking advantage of your size and strength? We do not tolerate older or bigger children hitting smaller youngsters: We call them bullies. Why should parents be able to do the same? Significantly, parents do not spank their older children. Is it because they fear that the youngsters might strike back?

Spanking can get out of hand. Anger is a powerful emotion. If you are in the habit of spanking, you run a greater risk of losing control, which could result in physical or emotional injury to your child. This frequently happens in some cases of child abuse *(page 59)*. Because there is such a risk, some people advise never to hit in anger. I concur. But I view premeditated spanking as being even less excusable than losing control.

Spanking injures the relationship between you and your child. Because a few young children hug their parents after being spanked, some people conclude that this is a sign of contrition and that the spanking does not affect the youngsters' love for them. But I see such children as earnestly trying to reestablish the loving and trusting relationship they so desperately need, which the spanking has just ruptured.

Spanking discourages cooperation. Personally, I am not apt to like a person who hits me, and while I will try to avoid being hit again, I will not go out of my way to cooperate with such an individual in the future. The same goes for children. They are not going to trust and cooperate with the parent who hits them, and you will need their cooperation to maintain control as the youngsters get older.

Spanking teaches the wrong lesson. Spanking teaches the child that when someone does something that is not liked, one hits them. That certainly is not a message our children and society need. The hypocrisy of spanking is never more evident than when a parent spanks a child for hitting a playmate.

Spanking as a general practice is not as effective as other disciplinary measures. If you want to discourage a specific, voluntary action, such as stopping your little girl from yanking your houseplants out of their pots, spanking will probably work. But in addition to creating the side effects that I have just listed, spanking generally is quite limited in its effectiveness as a disciplinary measure. It does nothing, for example, to instill in children the kind of positive behaviors that we would like to see them display — everything from politeness and concern for others to a willingness to settle disputes amicably.

If you avoid spanking, then what can you do? Recognize, first, that discipline means much more than punishment. Mainly, it means guidance, the promotion of appropriate, as opposed to inappropriate, social behaviors. So you should emphasize teaching the behaviors you want to encourage and congratulate your child for exhibiting them at least as often as you correct undesirable ones. The parents who never praise their children for behaving well are practicing what I call "squeaky-wheel discipline," in which the only time the children receive attention is when they get into trouble.

Some people argue that not spanking leads to no discipline at all. Those parents who plead with their children to behave, yell at them or issue threats they never carry out may actually be promoting disobedience. But avoiding spanking does not mean anything goes. Be prepared to apply the alternate methods of discipline described in this book. Plan ahead. Imagine those situations that are bound to arise and how you will deal with them. Write down the rules you wish followed and note what the consequences will be for violating them. This will help you to be consistent. Of course, your methods will require adjusting as your child matures. And you will not be able to anticipate everything: Children are very inventive. But you will be less likely to resort to spanking in the heat of the moment when you are prepared in advance to handle your youngster's behavioral problems thoughtfully and calmly.

Robert B. McCall, Ph.D.
Director, Office of Child Development
University of Pittsburgh

reinforcing his more positive actions with frequent praise.

In more difficult situations, enlightened parents can get the message across in no uncertain terms without ever resorting to corporal punishment of even the lightest kind. You can, for instance, ignore the child when his behavior leaves something to be desired. This removes from him the attention he craves, motivating him to change his ways. Then, too, you can let him discover the natural consequences of his actions, or withdraw special privileges or activities, or even briefly isolate him. All these punishments allow the child to come to grips with himself, without undue loss of dignity, and, used fairly, they ultimately instill in him respect for parental authority.

Of these four methods described below, use the one that fits your child and his particular misbehavior the best, but be sure to act promptly; any delay in carrying out the punishment is bound to dilute the effect you want it to have.

A child who has refused to put on her mittens experiences the consequence of her decision when her hands grow icy, forcing her to reconsider.

Ignoring

The mildest of punishments involves ignoring the offending behavior. By disregarding it, you are withdrawing the most sought-after reward your youngster can have — attention. Children, of course, flourish on it; to deprive them of it even briefly can have an immediate impact. The technique of ignoring is particularly effective when your youngster seems determined to irritate or shock you. Your deliberate failure to be fazed by her whining or her sudden use of an expletive is bound to give her pause. Without your anger or surprise to stimulate her, she will lose interest in her tactic. Once she has reversed herself, be sure to commend her for the turnaround.

When ignoring your youngster, be steadfast. If she is demanding a piece of chocolate and you feel she should not have one at the moment, tell her only once, "No candy now." Then look away so as to avoid having any eye contact with her and remain silent, despite her begging. This means not giving her even the slightest nonverbal cue. Smiling as though you secretly find her behavior cute will only encourage her. So will visibly tensing up, a sure sign to her that she is getting to you.

Your youngster may now use all her wiles to catch your attention, including running around the room, bouncing on the bed or rolling on the carpet. And some children react to being ignored by strenuously seeking physical contact with the parent. Your child may climb onto your lap, tug at your clothes or grab your leg. It may take an act of will on your part, especially when her little face displays unhappiness, but refuse to acknowledge her actions. Once she stops her shenanigans, however, start paying attention to her. If she becomes involved in an activity you approve of and she has dropped her demand for chocolate, begin to praise her: "Good, you're playing so nicely now. I like it when you keep yourself busy like that."

Some parents find it almost impossible to tune out a child's whining, crying or frantic tantrum, and they cave in. If you feel this happening, try removing yourself from the situation, providing your youngster is in no danger of harming herself. You might go into the bedroom or bathroom and wait there alone until she calms down.

Many parents have learned that they must use the technique of ignoring a couple of times to ensure that the behavior does in fact change. You may have to go through the process all over again day after day, as your child continues to test you. But if you persist in ignoring her behavior, you can be almost certain that it will disappear. Parents who give in make a mistake. When they do, they are only reinforcing the very behavior they want to eliminate. Ignoring is an all-or-nothing thing.

Natural consequences
The equally effective punishment called natural consequences obliges the child to accept the outcome of his behavior. For example, if your youngster dawdles over his food after being told not to, remove his plate when you take away the rest of the family's dishes. Should he ask for a snack later, be consistent and say no. He will soon realize that when he does not eat the food on his plate, he goes to bed hungry. Or if despite your advice, he refused to bring his favorite Teddy bear in from the garden before the rain started, tell him: "Since you left your bear outside in the rain, it's soaked. Now you'll have to find something else to sleep with tonight."

Experiencing cause and effect firsthand teaches children to

make realistic assessments of their actions. But since some youngsters may be too young to connect the unpleasant results with the deed, it is always important for you to underscore the link between the two and to explain as clearly and simply as possible the rationale behind the punishment they receive.

When using the method of natural consequences, do not let your anger degenerate into vindictiveness. Never proclaim, "You see? It serves you right for not listening to me!" Rather say, for example, "Let me bandage your knee, and then you can walk slowly instead of running so you won't trip and hurt yourself again." Resist any temptation to heap blame upon blame by bringing up previous incidents; address the issue at hand only.

Withdrawing privileges

An extension of natural consequences is the much used punishment, withdrawal of privileges. The point, of course, is to take away a privilege, a favorite activity, a toy or a game for a specific period. The punishment is easy enough to apply and teaches its lesson well. If, after being warned about the dangers, your youngster still darts into the street when playing with his friends, you have good reason to order him inside and tell him that he must play alone for half an hour. Or if he refuses to stop racing his tricycle down a steep and dangerous hill, locking up the tricycle in the garage for an afternoon will show him not only that you mean business, but that he must pay a penalty for ignoring you. When that lesson is learned, your child will think twice about repeating the behavior.

Since they are based on logic, both the removal of privileges and natural consequences require that you be fair and consistent in your application of the punishment. Make sure that the punishment always fits the circumstances and that it lasts no longer than need be. For your daughter's failure to straighten up her doll shelf, you might take away some of her dolls for an afternoon. For your son's repeated failure to scrape the mud off his shoes before coming into the house, withdrawing his right to watch television for a week is bound to strike him as an unduly severe penalty, as indeed it is. It would be more appropriate to tell the youngster that he will not be allowed to see his favorite show that evening.

How long should a prohibition last? Generally, a half hour to an hour works with younger children, an afternoon for older ones. Extending a prohibition unduly may only fuel your youngster's anger with you and prolong the behavior you want changed. Moreover, by stretching out the punishment, you are depriving yourself of an opportunity to teach your child the positive behavior she can begin to practice after the punishment is over. When too much time elapses, the child is no longer in a position to make the connection between cause and effect and your praise.

Time-out For children, time passes much more slowly than it does for adults, and this makes time-out, during which the youngster must sit or stand alone in a specific spot for a predetermined period, a particularly effective discipline technique. It is especially useful when such misbehavior as destroying property, hitting or antagonizing others physically or verbally is involved. It can also be very effective in a situation where you have given your youngster an instruction and he has refused to comply. For example, you may ask him to remove his toy cars from under the kitchen table. If he begins picking up the cars immediately, you can praise him for it. But if he balks at doing so, you should then say, "Time-out because you won't pick up those cars." Immediately lead the child to your time-out location. Always give a reason for instituting the punishment but make it short. Resist any temptation to interrogate or lecture the youngster, and brook no argument.

For his misbehavior, this youngster must sit alone on the stairs until the timer next to him goes off. The safe but boring experience acts as an immediate corrective.

The location for a time-out should be a dull but safe place that is in no way scary. Never use a closet or a dark room, which will only activate a child's fears and be a source of nightmares. For a toddler, it might be an empty hallway or a quiet room where you can watch him out of the corner of your eye. Even stationing him in a chair at the other end of the room where you happen to be will suffice. For an older youngster, use an uncluttered laundry room, a staircase or any other uninteresting spot. Do not place the offender where he can glimpse the TV or gaze out a window. Try to remove anything from the scene that his anger might lead him to throw or damage. If he kicks the wall, ignore him as long as the time-out lasts. In fact, studiously turn your back on all of his attempts to get your attention, so long as he stays where he is supposed to be.

If the child is quite young, you should escort him to the spot where the time-out is to occur and have him sit down. Make it clear to him why he must stay there; a simple statement such as "Time-out because you hit Mary" should do the trick.

A child who rebels against time-out should be escorted back

Parent to Parent

About Disciplining

66 Eric wouldn't wash his face when he got dressed in the morning, and it was a struggle when I tried to do it. One day, I saw a pig puppet washcloth in a store. I bought it, and the next morning I wet it and made the puppet say, 'Eric, you look so sleepy this morning, I'm going to bite your nose.' All the while I was washing the area around his nose. Eric took the puppet from me and began washing the rest of his face, carrying on a conversation with the puppet. After that, washing his face was his favorite part of the morning routine. 99

66 Larry was old enough to understand the meaning of 'no,' so I explained that his little rocking chair would be where he would have to sit when he misbehaved. After that, if I said no and he went on with what he was doing or had a screaming fit, I would sit him in his rocking chair for two minutes. At first I used a kitchen timer and set it, but when he got older, I told him he could tell me when he was ready to behave. Within 30 seconds, he would say 'I'm ready now.' Whenever he misbehaved, I would tell him it was wrong and why, warning him that the next time he did it he would have to sit in his chair. 99

66 At the end of a frazzled day when Laura is at her worst and so am I, we are sometimes too tense to resolve our differences calmly. So I just break through whatever is happening and say, 'I think you need a hug,' and I give her one. It dissolves the tension like magic. What's happening is she really does need a hug; in fact, we both need to touch and to reconnect on an elementary level. 99

66 Carl, my five-year-old, sometimes is in a bad mood when I get home from the office, and I ask, 'Did you have a bad day?' If he says something grumpy and continues acting up, I figure he wants to let me know he is mad but is not ready to tell me why. So I give him a bath, letting him play for 20 minutes with his toys in the water. Soon he is singing, playing and getting relaxed; usually by the time he's out of the tub he is able to open up to me. So whenever he gets bratty I think to myself, 'Water — it's time to try the soothing qualities of water.' 99

66 Janet is clever about challenging me. One day I realized she was trying to get me into a game that I could lose two ways: either by giving in to her or by screaming until she did what I wanted. I changed the rules of the game. Now if I tell her to pick up her toys and she says no, instead of getting into the struggle she is aiming for, I will say, 'You better do it or I'm going to get you.' Then she giggles and runs off while I chase her. I turned a confrontation into something fun that leaves both of us happy. Then there is a spirit of good will between us and she is cooperative. 99

66 Each of my boys was about two when I started using the old game: 'I want you to stop by the time I count to five.' By the count of three they would shape up even though I hadn't made any threat. But each child reached a stage when he had to test this and would wait to see what would happen after I counted to five. Then I had to give up the trick or warn them in advance of a punishment and be firm about sticking to it. 99

66 When I know I can be firm, I let John, three, feel the consequences of his negative actions. 'You don't want to wear your coat? Okay. We'll just take it along,' I say. Many times he's put on his coat on the sidewalk after feeling the chill. Or I might say: 'If you take too long getting ready for bed, there won't be time for a story.' When I stick to it — the hardest part — it usually works. 99

66 Sharon wouldn't get out of bed in the morning to go to day care. My husband and I bought her an alarm and set it to ring 15 minutes before she had to be up. We told her that if she got up when it rang, she could come and climb under the covers with us for 15 minutes and get up when we did. She loved doing that and jumped out of her bed whenever the alarm rang. 99

66 Good discipline happens when I can focus my full attention on the problem. But that's hard to do when I'm under pressure. For instance, when we are rushing to get out of the house in the morning and Cynthia hasn't put on her shoes or combed her hair, I have my mind on a whole range of things, so we often get into a screaming match. But if I stop for a minute and turn my full attention to her and say, 'Would you like to brush your hair or shall I?' I can get her to do what she should be doing. 99

66 I've discovered that by giving my little boy the choice of changing his behavior, I have much better luck getting him to do so. When I tell him to come right inside if he can't behave outside, I realize I'm giving him no alternative. But when I say something like, 'You can either play outside without hitting your friend, or you can play inside by yourself,' it works like a charm. 99

66 Marissa showed a sudden passion for using dirty words she picked up from other kids. I guess she was out to shock us. Rather than being surprised, I did what someone told me to do — I said to her, 'We don't talk to you like that, and we don't expect you to talk to us that way,' and I went into the other room. And you know, it worked. 99

to the spot as many times as necessary to convince him that you have no intentions of relenting. Should he persist, impose another consequence: "Because you can't stay in time-out, you will have to go to bed a half hour earlier tonight." And be sure to follow through.

Why time-out works
Time-out works partly because children dislike it so much. For one thing, it is boring. They would much prefer to be playing with toys or friends than having to remain quiet in one spot with nothing to do. Minutes can drag on for them and seem like hours. Because they do, make time-out short. Some parents key it to their youngster's age — a minute of time-out for each year of his life. For toddlers, thirty seconds is often sufficient.

So that your youngster will know when time-out is up, you might set a kitchen timer and tell him that if he sits quietly until the buzzer sounds, he can get up and leave; otherwise, time-out will be extended another minute. Or, if he is an older child, you can tell him that he may go when he himself decides that he can control his behavior. Once time-out is over, announce gently that the child is free to return to his activity.

If you have put the youngster in time-out for his failure to comply with your directions and if after time-out you repeat the command and he still refuses to obey, put him in time-out again. When he does comply, jump at the first opportunity you get to demonstrate your pleasure in his modified behavior.

The many uses of time-out
Time-out can be used on children who misbehave together. Follow the same procedure as you would for a single child, but separate the youngsters and place them where neither can see the other. Time-out may also be used with a toy to teach a lesson. It works well when two children are feuding over a play thing. Just pick up the toy, say that you are putting it away and then place it where they can see it but not get at it. Tell them that the toy is in time-out and that they can have it later, when they indicate that they are willing to share it.

The beauty of time-out is that it is a punishment that you can take with you — in a car, on a shopping expedition or on a vacation. You can put your child in a time-out in the back seat, in an unbusy spot in a supermarket or a department store, or a motel room. But whatever you do when you are away from home, do not leave your youngster alone. As with all these methods of punishment, collect yourself, be patient and look upon time-out as an opportunity to restore the equilibrium that will promote good behavior wherever you and your child happen to be. ❖

Dealing with Your Anger

Even the calmest of parents sometimes become angry at their children when they misbehave. This is a fundamental reality, and it is one that must be faced squarely. During tense or frustrating moments, it is all too easy to lash out at those closest to you — especially a child who has provoked or irritated you.

But the kind of violent anger that prompts you to yell at, berate, strike, shake or demean your youngster is not only likely to frighten him, but to leave him confused over your reckless use of power. What is more, in the aftermath of such a blowup parents can feel tremendous guilt that may then encourage them to try to make it up to their children, thus conveying a very mixed message. In some instances, the emotion fuels itself, quickly getting out of hand and leading to child abuse.

Certainly, you are not going to harm your youngster if occasionally you get angry with her. Anger is a very human emotion and no child should be shielded completely from it if she is to be able to cope with the people and situations she will confront in the world beyond the home. But it is the degree and frequency of the anger that matters and these should be controlled.

After an angry outburst, a mother apologizes to her son and explains the reason she lost her temper. By holding the child and speaking softly, she restores good feeling between the two of them.

How to get a grip on your anger

If you feel yourself becoming enraged, try to understand why before the emotion runs away with you. Pull back, if you can, and pause to reflect. Is the incident or problem truly worth getting so upset over? Are you really that angry at your child or are you instead troubled over something that happened to you during the day? Was his act more a healthy stretching of boundaries, essential to his development, than a deliberate provocation? By stopping to analyze the situation, you give yourself the opportunity to cool off. At such moments, the old technique of counting to 10 can help. Or try taking five deep breaths.

The feeling may not dissipate right away, in which case you can resort to several activities that may help dispel it. Go for a walk with your child, put on a favorite tape or radio station, or phone a friend. Time and circumstances permitting, take a soothing shower or a bath, stretch out on the couch or write down your reactions and thoughts.

At your most frazzled you may sometimes think that your youngster is deliberately out to get your goat. One way to gain control of yourself at such a moment is not to wonder "Why is she doing this to me?" but to think instead, "I wish she wouldn't do that — how can I teach her not to?" Such a shift in attitude may lead you to the real reason for her misbehavior. She may, in fact, be seeking desperately to gain your attention, even when this means winning your disapproval. If she is, consider how you can give her more attention of the right kind.

As busy parents know all too well, irrational anger is often the outgrowth of stress and fatigue. To avoid reaching the boiling point, contemplate engaging regularly in some stress-releasing activity such as yoga, body-building, dancing or jogging. And remember that the best of parents need an occasional break from their children, so do not feel guilty for taking one. When you spend time alone with your spouse or your friends, you are rejuvenating your spirit and making yourself a better parent.

What to say to your child when you are upset

Despite all your efforts to manage your anger, you will undoubtedly lose your temper from time to time. When you fly off the handle, try saying afterward to your youngster, "I'm sorry I yelled at you." Then, once you have a grip on yourself, tell him, "Since I don't feel so angry now, let me explain why we do not do what you did today." Explanations can go a long way toward defusing the situation and restoring equilibrium. Your child will appreciate your honesty, and in apologizing, you will have won more of his respect as well. He, in turn, will have learned a way to handle his own anger. ❖

When a Parent's Anger Becomes Abuse

Parental rage that turns habitually into an outpouring of screaming and violence against the child and inflicts physical or emotional damage is known as child abuse. It is often the result of extreme stress — unemployment, marital problems or personal setbacks. Parents who find themselves venting their frustrations over and over on their children may be unconsciously repeating the acts of abuse or neglect they suffered in their own childhoods. Often their expectations of child rearing may have been unrealistic in the first place, with little anticipation of the work entailed or the potential strains that they now feel they cannot handle. Child abusers come from all social, economic, racial, religious and ethnic backgrounds. In families where abuse occurs, both spouses may be active abusers, or one may be a more passive participant encouraging abusive acts or perhaps accepting and hiding them.

The guilt and depression that a parent may feel after an incident of child abuse can be as overwhelming as the rage that started it all; yet guilt does not prevent further incidents. A parent who strikes out over and over at his child when he is an-

gry at himself needs help. The best time to seek help is before there is a serious incident. If you find yourself lonely or frequently depressed, overwhelmed by day-to-day problems and frightened by the anger you sometimes feel toward your children, you may want to turn to one of many community agencies that offer professional guidance.

Help is available through mental-health clinics, community hot lines, local agencies and government social-service bureaus that either refer the parent who calls or deal with the problem directly, often by providing services to families in their own homes. Some parents who can afford private therapists prefer this form of aid, and there are also national organizations such as Parents Anonymous or Parents United that have local chapters to help child abusers cope with the problem.

Experts estimate that two thirds of all child-abuse cases go unreported. If you become aware of a child who is in danger and the abuse seems obvious, you can ask for an investigation by your state agency, usually called the Department of Social Services or Children and Family Services.

The Many Faces
of Misbehavior

Many parents can recognize their own youngster in the little angel in tennis shoes sitting opposite. Her halo is slightly askew — from the weight of all those angelic deeds, no doubt. She may have behaved just beautifully in the Sunday-school pageant and then come home to show you everything she knows about being contrary. She can be an absolute lamb at someone else's birthday party but make a chaos of her own mealtimes. She may throw tantrums now and again when she cannot have her way, and she has been known to haul off and bop a favorite playmate when she loses a tug of war over a special toy. What is going on here?

Growth and development, mostly. Like the majority of children, our sometimes fallen angel truly wants to behave in ways that please the people she loves and who love her. But that is quite a large order. At times her parents overwhelm her by asking too much, and she tunes them out for a little while. Occasionally, they make a great fuss about behaving in a certain way and then somehow fail to notice how hard she is trying. And sometimes she has more important things on her mind than following some silly rule; there is a whole world out there to explore, and she is in a hurry to get on with it.

Mothers and fathers, of course, cannot stand aside. You will want to assess your child's behavior continually, determine why she is misbehaving — which is not always as obvious as it may seem — and deal with the situation in ways that correct specific problems without damaging your youngster's sense of self-worth or initiative. Most misbehavior is remarkably easy to handle, once you understand the whys and wherefores; then you need only show your child a better way, a more socially acceptable way, and chances are she will take it — sensible small person that she is.

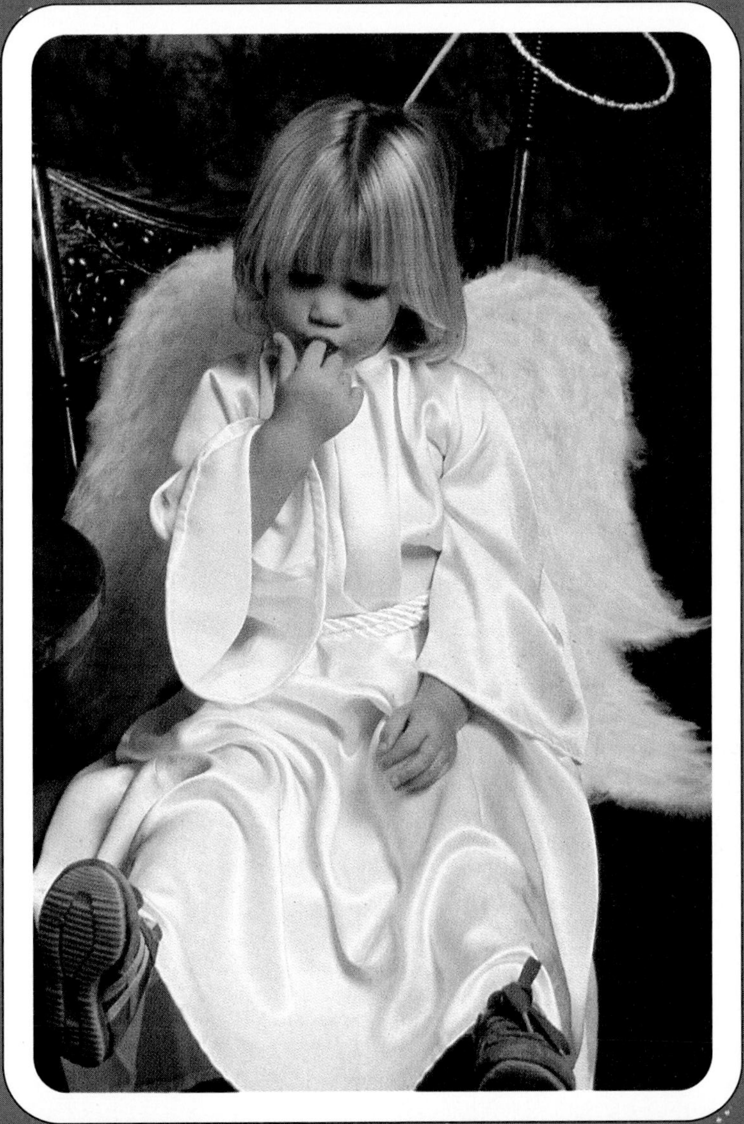

Understanding the Whys

An important aspect of teaching good behavior is keeping the bad behavior in perspective. This goes beyond simply realizing that misbehavior is a normal part of growing up. It means looking for the reasons for problem behavior: Why the tantrum in the grocery store? Why the rude behavior at dinner? Why all the dawdling on the way to bed? If you can figure out the motives for your child's behavior, you can often find better ways to deal with the problems. Experts agree that misbehavior is seldom purely random: It nearly always serves a purpose for the child.

The most obvious reasons for misbehavior are hunger, fatigue and illness. If you watch out for these problems — for example, by providing afternoon snacks, making sure that naptimes are routinely observed and being vigilant for symptoms of illness — you can minimize their impact on your youngster's behavior. Less obvious explanations for poor behavior include the child's need for parental attention, simple curiosity, misguided notions about how to win friends, family turmoil, bad example in the home, sibling rivalry and feelings of anger or frustration.

Reading your own reactions

In trying to decipher the reasons for your child's troubles, you sometimes have to analyze the situation on an emotional level as well as on an intellectual one. In the face of most incidents of bad behavior, you will feel some antagonism. But you may have other reactions as well, and these can be valuable clues to what your child is feeling at the time. If the youngster is simply trying to get your attention — as is very common — your feelings may be tinged with annoyance. If the child's misdeeds are an attempt to assert herself and give herself a sense of control, her actions may leave you feeling vaguely threatened. If she shouts at you or calls you a name, she is acting out anger or frustration and you will likely feel hurt. Use these feelings as part of your analysis of what is going on between the child and you.

Seeking attention through misbehavior

Perhaps the most common motive for misbehavior is the desire for attention from the parents. Children naturally seek attention as part of becoming social beings. They constantly try to reaffirm that they belong and are accepted, often in ways that are thoroughly beguiling and inventive. But they also seek attention in ways that are not so appealing. Showing off at family gatherings, throwing temper tantrums in the midst of your morning routine, asking endless questions that go far beyond the bounds of normal intellectual curiosity, fighting with siblings while you try to cook dinner — all of these may be nothing more than bids for attention. A passive child may also resort to helplessness. For example, a youngster who insists on help with her clothes after she is able to dress herself may simply be craving attention.

To the child, any response at all — even nagging, scolding or spanking — may seem better than being ignored. As a result, you may find that efforts to curb this attention-seeking behavior are frequently counterproductive; they may actually encourage the problem. You may also discover that some such behavior is more or less fully intentional. Your four- or five-year-old may giggle or smile sheepishly if you pick her up and tell her that you know why she acts that way. A toddler, of course, will not be so aware of her motives. In any case, your best bet is simply to see the behavior for what it is and to respond to it matter-of-factly.

Clambering onto his father's shoulder, this child takes a direct approach to getting attention. Many different forms of childish behavior — from baby talk to bickering — may be roundabout bids for parental attention.

Curiosity and testing limits

Curiosity fuels the process of learning. It is a natural and healthy impetus to explore the world. Curiosity also creates problems, however. Household treasures get broken in the hands of curious toddlers. Orders get overshadowed by enthusiasm to explore. Children sometimes even bite or use profanity just to see what results. Such problems notwithstanding, it is a bad idea to discourage curiosity in hopes of improving behavior. It is better to promote inquisitiveness within clear boundaries: "You can look at Mom's jewelry box, but I have to be there with you." It also helps to establish safe places for the youngster to explore — junk drawers, for example, or a catchall box that exists just for this purpose.

One nearly universal display of curiosity is in testing the limits set by parents. You should expect your child to challenge your rules. She is gathering answers to many different questions: Will this rule be enforced? Is this what I cannot do? Does the rule apply now or just at home? But these are all different aspects of the same basic issue: Where does my control begin and end? That issue looms large as children learn their own identity, and it shapes a portion of their daily behavior. Your role is to enforce the rules consistently. In that way, the child gradually grows able to predict the results as she experiments.

A need to be the boss

Some children turn the limits-testing phase into a genuine battle for power. "No, you can't make me!" becomes the stock response, often many times in a day. Contradicting, arguing, refusing to cooperate and other minor acts of rebellion characterize this variety of behavior. Such conduct sometimes grows out of attention seeking, with the child graduating to more confrontational tactics. Unfortunately, it is easy to reinforce this behavior unwittingly, because the motives behind it are often unclear. For example, a child who is refused a cookie may provoke a heated exchange with her mother. Even if the child does not get the cookie, she may continue being defiant because she savors the ability to get her mother excited.

It is usually best to answer resistance with calm, controlled action. "No, you may not watch television and we will not talk about it anymore." Stick to what you decide and refuse to get into lengthy discussions.

Fighting for turns on the rocking horse, these siblings, like most, spend quite a bit of time hashing out their respective rights and roles within the family.

Sibling rivalry

In the majority of cases, you can expect clashes between siblings. It is a normal part of establishing places in the family while learning to get along. Some experts hold the view that sibling rivalry serves a useful purpose in developing such skills as conflict solving, negotiation and fairness. The resulting conflicts, however, can produce a good deal of unpleasant behavior — notably teasing, physical aggression, arguments over possessions and back-seat spats.

Since you probably cannot eliminate sibling rivalry entirely, the issue comes down to where to draw the line: Where is the behavior normal and unavoidable, and where does it exceed acceptable bounds? The answer will vary from family to family. Many parents try to stay out of the squabbles as far as is practical, preferring to let the children solve their own disputes. You should certainly intervene, however, when a younger sibling is being bullied unreasonably or when there is danger of injury. Overall, you have to make it clear that you expect cooperation, and you must teach children how to get along by modeling the behaviors you like and giving praise when you see them performed.

Other family influences

A notable change in your child's behavior, particularly one that is sudden, may reflect changes in your family situation that are causing the youngster concern. Analyze recent events in her life, looking for significant disruptions that could be the root of such worries. Common difficulties such as moving, starting a new school and meeting new playmates are stressful to even the most well-adjusted child. Your patience and understanding will go a long way toward helping her get through these times. More severe crises, including a divorce, death or serious illness in the family, may require professional assistance as well.

Other problem behaviors may simply reflect actions the youngster sees at home. Yelling, lying, complaining and bad language are typical copycat crimes. In addition, a child who is frequently spanked may learn to be physically aggressive toward her playmates. Your child mimics you in all things. You can probably recall occasions when you have recognized your mannerisms or speech patterns acted out in the child's play. So you should not be surprised when that modeling carries over into behavior of yours that you do not wish to see imitated.

Trying to win friends

For the preschooler, who is just learning how to interact with her peers, social acceptance may become a powerful motive for behavior. Most often this impulse shows itself in the desire to have the same toys and wear the same clothes as other children. But in addition to bringing out instincts for conformity, uncertainty about the ins and outs of friendship may lead to acts such as stealing from siblings in order to get gifts with which to win favor. Some preschoolers also tell tall tales to impress their peers. Children need guidance about friendship: They may need to be taught that they can make friends without such tactics.

Feelings of anger or frustration

Some misbehavior results from anger and frustration, which at times are overwhelming to children. In many cases, frustrations arise when little ones are asked to do things beyond their capacities. Biting, teasing and angry outbursts toward parents are typical expressions of a child's inability to handle such pressures. When emotions run high, children generally feel hurt and often respond by trying to hurt those around them. Strong statements such as "I hate you" are painful to hear but are not uncommon. The child is expressing emotions in the only way she knows. She must be taught more-appropriate forms of expression.

Annoying developmental behaviors

Remember that some behaviors have no motives. A problem such as pants-wetting is inconvenient, but it is also unintentional. Clinging is likewise a developmental behavior, one that reflects the limits of a youngster's understanding. Other unappealing forms of behavior, such as thumb sucking, nose picking and masturbation, may begin as responses to fatigue and stress but quickly become habit, pure and simple. It is a mistake to label them as misbehavior. In general, such problems require patience rather than correction. When they disappear it is usually due to physical and emotional growth, though reassurance may help. Your attitude — relaxed and supportive — will do more to inspire change than coercion, nagging or punishment.

If you become concerned about such behavior's continuing too long, look for means of helping the child relax in socially acceptable ways. But also take notes on the specifics of the child's bad habit: when and where it occurs; its frequency; whether it seems to be increasing or decreasing. Your notes will help you describe the problem should you find it necessary to consult your pediatrician.

Pants-wetting

Nothing is more unappealing than wet, soggy pants, but the youngster usually cannot help this problem. Bed-wetting, in particular, indicates that a child is not developmentally ready to stay dry all night. Although some two- and three-year-olds acquire the regrettable habit of simply waiting too long to head for the toilet, most daytime accidents are also beyond control. Among the possible causes are overexcitement, stress and regression brought on by the arrival of new siblings. Occasional wetting between the ages of three and six is normal. Continual wetting at four years of age or frequent wetting that reappears unexpectedly may indicate a physical problem and should be called

Although she is embarrassed by her failure to reach the toilet in time, this three-year-old youngster is still at an age when occasional accidents are to be expected.

to the attention of your doctor. Children develop different skills at different ages: Toilet training is no exception.

Thumb sucking and other comfort habits

Thumb sucking, rocking back and forth before falling asleep, nose picking and twiddling the hair are classic examples of babyish security devices that evolve into unconscious habits. In general, such habits disappear by the age of five or six, with or without your attention. If you find that your child sucks his thumb at particular times of the day, try changing his routine. You might also use a star chart *(page 49)*.

Though embarrassing to parents when performed in public, masturbation and self-exploration are a normal part of growing up and should not be viewed with alarm. Masturbation may begin as early as 18 months. It tends to peak between the ages of three and five, then diminishes in frequency until puberty. You can teach a child who is three and a half years of age or older that this is private behavior. With a younger child, your best hope is to try to divert his attention.

Reliable, custom-fit, always accessible — the thumb is the comfort habit of choice for this little girl. Calling attention to such habits may only add tension and thus make them harder to abandon.

Clinging and baby talk

Clinging and becoming distraught upon separation from parents are phases that most children go through. Many babies become wary of strangers at the age of about nine months, which may signal the start of these tendencies. Clinging is fairly common up to three years of age; it waxes and wanes between three and four, happens occasionally at four and is almost entirely gone by five. It is very unusual in older children but may result from changes in routine or from traumatic events or particular feared situations, such as getting a shot at the doctor's office. When a youngster begins clinging in response to trauma, such as a death in the family, you must help her find ways to cope with the grief, and you may need professional assistance to do so.

Reverting to baby talk is usually a way of seeking attention, but it may not be a conscious strategy on the part of the child. The common precipitator is the arrival of a new sibling, who has temporarily pushed the youngster out of the spotlight. When this is the case, the baby talk is usually short-lived, but you can hasten its end by making it clear to the child that she must ask for things in a grown-up voice or you will not listen to her. A child who habitually speaks in an infantile fashion and has never shown more advanced speaking ability may have a physical disability. If you suspect such a condition, consult your doctor. ⁙

When Problem Behavior Gets Out of Hand

Families who are experiencing significant pathological problems — in cases where children are retarded or emotionally disturbed, for example, or where parents tend to abuse their youngsters or cannot cope with alcohol or depression — should of course seek professional treatment. Yet no matter how well-adjusted or patient or loving parents may be, a small minority of otherwise normal children will develop behavior problems that require help outside the home. If your child has severe or persistent troubles, you will need to know where to look for assistance and how to choose an appropriate problem-solving approach.

Before seeking help, be certain that you need it *(box, opposite)*. Bear in mind that parents commonly feel frustrated or even overwhelmed in the face of behavior problems. It may be that you are expecting too much too soon from your preschooler. More often than not, the difficulties are short-lived and disappear without professional intervention. If you suspect that there are genuine problems, however, do not hesitate; these troubles are best dealt with while your child is young.

Where to find help Explain your concerns to your pediatrician first. Pediatricians are good sounding boards because they observe so many children. What is more, some pediatricians are now trained in behavioral pediatrics and are treating children with minor problems. However, if your doctor does not practice such therapy or seems overly inclined to attribute all difficulties to a "stage the child is going through," get a second opinion. Aside from treatment, the doctor's role should be to rule out possible physical causes, then, based on your descriptions of what is going wrong, to recommend appropriate social agencies or private counselors. Other good sources of advice are the teachers at your child's nursery school, community health centers, hospital referral services and child-guidance specialists in the public schools.

Counselors trained to help with behavior problems include psychiatrists, psychologists and clinical social workers. Make sure that the therapist is experienced in working with children and is licensed by the state; the quality of care your child receives should be your primary concern. Furthermore, most insurance companies do not cover unlicensed therapists.

You may wish to interview a number of therapists before selecting one for your child. Look for someone who is willing to answer your questions and also seems likely to establish rapport with your youngster. Ask about the therapist's methods of treatment — in particular, whether the family is brought into the process. Discuss cost, frequency of visits and, after the therapist has had a chance to evaluate the child, how long the treatment can be expected to continue. Once you have chosen a course of action, you should establish at the outset when you will meet with the therapist to assess the effectiveness of the treatment. Most experts recommend two weeks after the initial session. Some change in behavior should be evident in about a month; if not, you may want to consult another therapist.

Approaches to problem behavior

Professionals usually take one of three primary approaches to behavioral difficulties. One of these, play therapy, focuses on the child alone, with the therapist using games and exercises to get to the bottom of the child's concerns; but this is the least common method and not the most effective, in the opinion of many experts. A more direct approach is family therapy, in which parents and child meet with the therapist to talk through the troubles and search for explanations. This method is favored by therapists who regard poor behavior as a symptom of other family problems. In the third approach, parenting skills therapy, the therapist concentrates on teaching the parents how to deal with particular behavior problems in the home environment.

To reassure your child as he embarks on therapy, you can describe the therapist as a person who helps families that are not as happy as they would like to be. During the treatment, watch for signs that the youngster feels at ease with his counselor but do not be overly concerned if he sometimes seems uncomfortable; he may simply be at a critical point in the therapeutic process and feel tense about it. If he is reluctant to continue, discuss it with the therapist. Above all, be sure to follow through at home on the therapist's advice. ⋰

An Expert's View

Signs That Professional Help Is in Order

There is no obvious dividing line between the troubled child and the youngster who is simply rebellious or difficult by temperament. The differences are generally ones of tone or degree. There are, however, a few clear warning signs that indicate you should probably seek expert advice:

- Inability to adjust. At three or older, the child's general lack of discipline seems to interfere with acceptance by his peers.
- Anger in response to discipline. The child refuses to abide by time-outs and responds belligerently to other disciplinary measures. His reactions may include tantrums or physical aggression that is disproportionately intense given the nature of the original misbehavior.
- Antisocial patterns. The child consistently misbehaves, and efforts to change his behavior are not effective.
- Sleep problems. At four years of age or older, the youngster experiences severe bedtime anxiety that lasts for 90 minutes or

longer, or he frequently awakens in fear during the night.
- Prolonged periods of unhappiness. Either you or your child is continually unhappy because of tensions arising from the youngster's behavior. When the child is five or six, you may notice a pattern of self-deprecating remarks, such as, "I'm a bad boy," or "I do lots of naughty things."
- The child is in command. The balance of power has effectively shifted so that your youngster, not you, determines bedtimes and schedules for other activities, such as eating.
- Notice from the child's school. It is not likely that a youngster will behave worse at school than he does at home, but you may not recognize the seriousness of a discipline problem until the school brings it to your attention.

Edward R. Christophersen, Ph.D.
Department of Pediatrics
Kansas University Medical Center

A Catalogue of Misbehaviors

Good behavior is a matter of learning and abiding by social rules. Children are born willing and able to learn, and they crave the parental approval that favorable conduct brings. But learning rules is often difficult for the very young, because such small children are neither emotionally nor intellectually equipped to comprehend the reasons behind social conventions. They have to accept much of it on faith — not easy at any age. Consequently, they do not learn rapidly, and they have trouble linking one experience to another. Just because your toddler understands that biting is unacceptable does not mean that she will draw the same conclusion about fighting or throwing things. Each set of rules has to be acquired separately, and that happens only with a great deal of repetition.

Your job as a parent is to be patient, forbearing and very precise in getting the rules across. Try to be specific in your demands and imaginative in the ways that you model the behaviors you want your child to adopt. Be willing to tolerate the inevitable lapses that will occur and always be ready to offer praise for the young one's efforts as well as her successes. It cannot be stated too often: Praise is a better motivator than punishment.

The catalogue that begins here and ends on page 91 is by no means comprehensive; your preschooler will find any number of ways to test your forbearance. The most common problems are organized into four broad sections: Pages 70-76 deal with annoying habits, such as negativism, whining and interrupting; pages 77-83 cover problems in the daily routines of dressing, eating and bedtime, and in ventures out in public; pages 83-89 include the more aggressive behaviors, such as teasing, biting and throwing things; and pages 90-91 discuss lying, cheating and stealing. In each case, there is a description of possible causes for the misbehavior and a discussion of measures you can take to correct it or, even better, prevent it in the first place. References are made occasionally to the use of time-out and other specific discipline techniques; those are discussed in detail on pages 50-57 of this book.

Negativism

Why It Happens

Young children have a tendency to say "no" constantly. Small wonder: It is a word they hear all too often from their parents. Youngsters make "no" serve a number of purposes. It is a wonderful nonsense word, with a short, vigorous sound that the beginning talker can roll cheerfully over his tongue in strings of "no, no, no." At this stage, defiance and negativism are the furthest things from his mind. The loud "No!" that actually does convey defiance comes at around the 15th month, when your little one is developing a more distinct sense of self. His need for assertion is a healthy sign of growing independence. The reasonable "no," the one he uses to express personal preferences much as you do, appears around the age of three, along with all sorts of other, not-so-reasonable negative phrases, such as: "I won't," "I don't," and "I can't."

What to Do

Negativism becomes a problem only if you allow yourself to be maneuvered into a confrontation. You will exacerbate the situation by reacting angrily to your child's "No!" The best way to avoid being trapped by him is to let him say "no," but make it quite clear that he must nevertheless do as you ask because you know what is best. You may say, "I'm sure you do not want to take your bath, but you have to take it, and when you have finished, you may play your game again." This lets your youngster know that you sympathize with his objections, but that you are not budging from your position. At the same time, you should make a practice of reacting positively when you see affirmative behavior. Smile and offer your child praise: "That was such a nice 'yes' you said. I really like to hear you say that word!" You may also find that it helps to avoid asking your youngster questions that require yes-or-no answers. The rhetorical, "Shall we go now?" when you really mean, "Time for us to go," is just begging for trouble.

Tantrums

Why They Happen

A temper tantrum erupts when a child becomes so over-whelmed with anger or frustration that she loses all self-control. While every youngster occasionally succumbs to such outbursts, it is the so-called difficult child who has them most frequently and intensely. Tantrums are common between 18 months and three years of age, a period during which a child is rapidly discovering new skills — and with them, a tantalizing new sense of freedom. When confronted with limits to this independence — either because of parental interference or her own physical and intellectual limitations — a tempestuous child may explode as often as once or twice a day. Though the causes may seem trivial, one way or another the child has reached the limits of her tolerance. She may kick, scream, cry or hold her breath until she turns blue.

Parents often overreact, either pleading with the child to stop, shouting or angrily shaking her. Worse yet, some promise to capitulate if their child will simply stop. Even if the first few tantrums were unintentional, a child treated this way soon realizes that interesting things happen when she loses her temper. She gets attention, and best of all, she may even get what she wants. Had the parental reaction been different, the tantrums would probably have disappeared gradually. As it is, she may begin to have them more frequently.

What to Do

To reduce and gradually eliminate temper tantrums, you should simultaneously pursue both short- and long-term strategies. Foremost, you should ignore the tantrums when they happen. Do not approach your little screamer, try to reason or argue with her or even speak to her while the tantrum is in progress. And put on your best poker face; try not to let your expression betray the least bit of concern. This will require some effort, but remember that your child depends on reactions from you to fuel her tantrums.

You should, however, remain in the room while the tantrum is going on — busying yourself with something else. A tantrum is likely to frighten your child as deeply as it affects you, so your presence is important. If her tantrum is so disruptive that it bothers other people, or if others are providing an audience, simply pick her up and carry her someplace where she can continue her tantrum in private. In the event the child starts to knock things over in her fury, calmly but firmly say: "Time-out.

No throwing or pushing." Then make her take a quick time-out, sitting right where she is on the floor. Do not let her move until she calms down.

When the tantrum is over, offer reassurance. Sit with her until she has recovered, then say: "I'm glad you are feeling better now. You really felt angry, I know. But I don't like yelling and screaming so I had to stop listening." When she is composed, involve her in some simple activity she enjoys.

An important part of your long-range strategy is to identify the things that trigger your child's tantrums, so that when you see trouble brewing you can step in and calmly offer to help. You might say, "I'll bet we can make this truck roll better if we try to do it this way."

You also want to teach alternative ways of handling frustration and anger. Be on the lookout for any behavior that suggests progress and let your child know how pleased you are. If an end to play has been provoking tantrums and she happens to come willingly this time, you might say, "You make me very proud by coming in so cheerfully when I call. I'm going to let you play longer tomorrow just for that."

You might also try explaining how you manage your own feelings, modeling the right ways to cope with stress and citing situations that she can understand. The next time you find yourself in a traffic jam, try not to fume or pound on the steering wheel: Your outbursts make a deep impression on the child. Instead, you might say, "I get angry when we have to wait like this, but then I just turn on some nice music and say to myself, 'What's the hurry anyway?'" You may be exaggerating, but the point is worth making.

If your youngster's tantrums occur more than two or three times a day, or if they seem to be increasing rather than diminishing in frequency and length despite your attempts to correct the behavior, then you should seek professional advice. And of course get help if the tantrums ever seem on the point of endangering your child.

Disobedience

Why It Happens

Your youngster is bound to disobey you. The only questions are how often, at what ages, under what circumstances and with what effect on you. A very young child often disobeys out of confusion or lack of understanding: She just cannot process all the information she needs to carry out your orders. She may also be unable to see the reason for your rules because she is looking at the world from a viewpoint that centers on herself and her needs; your priorities are not yet hers.

Then, too, she may be so absorbed in some activity that she does not hear you with full awareness, even though she may be looking straight at you. Unlike adults, who can attend to several things at once, a two- or three-year-old operates pretty much on one track. As your youngster gets older and a little more sure of herself, she also becomes enthralled by the urge to explore and investigate — and this urge can take precedence over your admonitions to "keep away from there" or "leave that alone." If she has a naturally independent turn of mind — and some children begin to assert themselves at a remarkably early age — she may defy you merely as an expression of her independence.

What to Do

Children thrive on structure and order; they like rules and predictability. You should decide on a reasonable set of priorities, determining which rules are of primary importance and which matters can often be left to choice. Your most important rules will have to do with basic safety measures and day-to-day routines, such as sitting at the table until meals are finished and going to bed on time. But you can give your little one considerable say in what toy she wants to play with, which activity she wants to do first, what clothes she wants to wear and so on.

You should start teaching compliance with rules when your toddler is between 15 and 18 months old. A first step is to explain something you want her to do, then follow words with actions. You might say, "Now is the time to come to the table." If she does not understand or says no, you should gently take her by the hand and lead her to the table. She will soon learn that you mean business. You can reinforce cooperative behavior by praise and a tangible reward: "Good, now that you're at the table, you may have your juice."

As your child grows older and starts exercising her independence, you will want to match your rules and requests to her ability to follow them. First, you should gauge how many instructions she is able to hold in her head at once, something you can determine by playing a little game when she is in a cooperative mood. Ask her to "get the ball, put it on the table and sit down next to me" and see whether she can complete all three tasks in the order you gave them. If her memory seems adequate but she has a hard time following directions anyway, try practicing direction-following skills as a game from time to time. Praise each success generously.

Stand close to your child and look at her directly when you are making a request or issuing a prohibition. That may mean stopping what you are doing to establish close eye contact first. Be pleasant about it. Do not say, "Look at me!" in an angry voice; children respond no better to bossiness than adults do. You might gently take your youngster's arm, instead, and say in a calm tone, "I want you to look at me now and listen to what I am going to say to you."

Make your requests clear and specific and always begin them by saying the child's name. Edie certainly knows what you mean when you say, "Edie, don't kick the dog," but a vague order to "be nice" when she is harassing the family pet invites her to make her own interpretation — which may not correspond to yours. Indeed, little Edie may not think that being nice has any bearing on what her foot is doing. Instead, tell the youngster clearly what not to do and give her a positive alternative: "Pat the doggie on the back."

Set time limits on your requests; when your youngster is misbehaving and you require immediate action, pause long enough for your child to cooperate on her own, but not too long. Child-discipline experts have found that a 10-second pause is about right — long enough to permit the slow-moving but cooperative youngster to act, but not so long as to give a noncompliant child the notion that she is winning a test of parental patience. When the 10 seconds are up and your child has not obeyed, issue an if-then warning, such as, "If you don't stop kicking the leg of the table, then I will put you in time-out." If she then obeys, compliment her; if not, promptly carry through with the discipline you promised. When she has paid the appropriate penalty, return her without comment to the situation she was in and give her another chance to cooperate. Be sure to praise her if she does. Naturally, do not employ the 10-second pause if she is doing something that endangers herself or others; in that event, intervene immediately.

When a child is younger than three, the time-out technique will not always gain compliance; the child forgets the task she is supposed to do as she gets involved in the authority struggle. The strategy of differential attention is often effective at this stage. This means paying attention to certain behaviors, but not to others. You might say calmly, "We'll just have to stand here until you brush your teeth." And then ignore all behavior other than tooth-brushing, focusing on the fact that her teeth have to be brushed before she gets to do anything else. You may have to wait awhile to get results the first time you try this, but subsequent attempts should work more promptly. Begin to praise her as soon as she starts toward the task; afterward go to a new activity that is fun to do.

When the emphasis is on completing a task such as cleanup, allow enough warning time before your child has to begin work so that she can finish what she is doing. You might say, "Five minutes until cleanup. I'll set a timer. When the timer goes off, it's time to clean up your toys. When you get your toys cleaned up, you can have your afternoon snack."

Whenever possible, emphasize the positive things you want your youngster to do instead of the negative things she should not do. The child who is told, "Play ball anywhere you like in the backyard, but you must stay in the backyard," is likely to feel a greater sense of freedom, and thus be less inclined to rebel, than if you say, "Don't play ball in the front yard." And the youngster who is told, "Ask me to put your record on the stereo when you want to hear it; but do not try to put a record on by yourself," will take the news better — and perhaps even keep her hands off that tempting piece of equipment — than the one who is told flatly, "You may not use the stereo."

Include a reason for your requests from time to time so that your child understands that rules and prohibitions are based on order and logic. Tell your preschooler, "Please put on your boots, because it is too cold for sneakers." At first, you should keep the explanations short and focused on a concrete fact. When your child gets older, she may be able to handle more abstract arguments, such as: "Your feet will get cold and spoil your afternoon."

And finally, you should make it a rule of yours that you make demands on your child only when you are willing to take the time and energy to follow through. If you cannot give those extra minutes to back up what you are asking your child to do, it is far better not to make the request at all.

Whining and Complaining

Why It Happens

Whining is talking in a helpless, dejected voice. In some children, this tone of voice appears like clockwork when the youngster is feeling out of sorts — with the beginnings of a cold, say, or an upset stomach. But children also whine when they are tired, bored, frustrated or annoyed. It is as if they could not muster the energy to produce ordinary, pleasant-sounding talk, or enough strength for a real bout of crying that would clearly express their discontent. Whining is all the more prevalent because it is certain to capture attention. Most parents find the sound highly annoying, and the instinctive reaction often is to do anything to placate the whiner. That, of course, does nothing but reinforce the sad-sounding talk. Whining rises to the level of a behavior problem when it becomes the youngster's regular mode of expression. And it is an easy habit to fall into if nothing is done to discourage the practice.

A companion problem, one that springs from many of the same causes, is incessant complaining. Preschoolers may go through spells of negativism when they are liable to find fault with everything around them. "I don't like chicken." "What are these black spots?" "How come it's so hot?" "Why can't we watch TV while we eat?" The complaints may or may not be delivered in a whining tone. And your child may not be appeased by your attempts to answer him. He may feed on the chance to complain even more.

What to Do

The trick to dealing with rampant complaining is not to let yourself get lured into the game. Simply refuse to respond to your youngster's lamentations. Explain that if his attitude remains so unpleasant, you will not talk with him. Then stick to it.

Dealing with whining demands similar resolve, but it also requires a certain amount of delicacy. When a child who is generally cheerful and compliant suddenly begins to whine, look for transient physical and emotional problems. Has your youngster gone short of sleep? Does he have a fever? Has it been too long since the last meal or snack? Redouble your efforts to be punctual about his

eating and sleeping schedules. In that way, you may eliminate some of the problems that have provoked the whining. If the crush of daily events is squeezing out time that you would normally devote to your preschooler, give the occasional whiner more of your time and attention, but do it in a general way throughout the day rather than in direct response to the whining. And consider whether any of the routines that the youngster depends on have undergone a significant shift. Is there a new baby? Father or mother away for a few days? Someone in the family sick or troubled? Some children are like weather vanes, responding to the slightest change around them.

If your child becomes a habitual whiner, you should look even more carefully for the reasons. It may be that you are subjecting him to demands that are either unreasonably high or ill-defined and thus poorly understood. Experts believe this sort of whining is more than just a bid for attention: It is a legitimate call for help or guidance. Make certain that your child knows what whining is, so that he will understand you if it becomes unreasonable and you tell him to stop. You might then explain that you cannot understand him when he whines; discuss things in terms of his "strong voice" or his "big-boy voice." Say to him, "Here is the way I would like you to ask for things." Then give an example, such as: "May I have a cookie, please?"

In the midst of a period of frequent whining, be sure to praise the times he speaks as he should: "When you speak nicely, I can understand you!" When possible, underscore your praise by giving him the item he requests. At the same time, you will want to make it a rule that whining will not result in what he wants, no matter how many times he whines for it. You may even have to walk out of the room. When you rejoin your youngster — or he rejoins you — pay close attention to his tone of voice and be generous in your approval if he speaks in a firm voice: "It is so nice to be with you when you are talking in your strong voice."

If your child is a chronic whiner, examine how you may have contributed to the problem. Do you give clear signals about the sorts of behavior you expect in given situations? Or perhaps you oversimplify instructions, saying, "Be a good boy," when he really does not know what you want him to do or not to do. It may be that you have to make certain basic changes in your way of relating to your youngster.

Above all, do not try to fight whining with threats or punishments. That approach offers little hope of success. And be careful not to present the model of an adult complainer or whiner. Even though you may not see any connection, your youngster may wonder why it seems to be okay for you but not for him.

Talking Back

Why It Happens

Name-calling, shouted retorts and defiance are normal, if bothersome, forms of rudeness that can appear any time after your youngster has learned to speak more or less fluently. They are particularly common to four- and six-year-olds, who are going through stressful periods of physical and mental development. Such rudeness does not often appear out of the blue; something usually happens to precipitate it. Perhaps you have told your child to do something he does not want to do, or he wants to do something but you have said no. Until he learns to communicate his feelings more maturely, rudeness may be his way of expressing anger, frustration and disappointment.

What to Do

Try not to rise to the bait when your child talks back. Many parents unconsciously become models of discourtesy by responding to rude children with shouts of anger: "Stop that this minute!" "I'll fix you!" Or worst of all: "I'll teach you not to talk to me that way." In fact, that is exactly what you are teaching him to do. However much you are provoked, ignore all but the most flagrant forms of back talk. Say, "I don't listen to talk like that." Keep a keen ear open for responses that are even the least bit agreeable and praise them. If your preschooler regularly traffics in "no" and "I hate you," then even a grudging "okay" is an improvement.

In the heat of the moment, be careful not to lose sight of the problem that provoked the outburst. If a child shouts, "I'm not going to pick up my toys, you dummy," do not get so distracted by the insult that you forget about the toys. The first priority is to make the child comply. Say, "It's your job to pick them up," or "Time-out for not listening."

When your angry little man calms down and seems ready to listen, talk to him pleasantly about acceptable ways to express his feelings. Explain that it is okay for him to tell you of his anger, but he should do it in a way that is not rude or hurtful. Demonstrate your point by saying, "I don't like it," first in an angry voice, then in gentle, matter-of-fact tones. After asking him which he likes to hear better, explain that you feel the same.

Profane Language

Why It Happens

Sometime around her fourth birthday, your child will probably discover a rich vocabulary of bathroom words. She may revel in hurling phrases such as "you big doo-doo" at her playmates, feeling witty and bold in the act. Her playmates will probably return the insults in kind and the fun will repeat itself harmlessly until the novelty wears off, usually within a few months. So-called dirty words and swear words, once learned, are primarily valued for their power to shock. They are not likely to find long-lasting use unless you make a big fuss about them. One other certain way to make profanity a problem is to use it yourself.

What to Do

To minimize the occurrence of bathroom language and swear words, be careful how you express yourself in front of your child. Avoid slang for anatomical parts or bodily functions. You do not want to imply by your figures of speech that a penis or feces are embarrassing or disgusting subjects that can only be talked about in code words. Try not to swear in the child's presence. If you forget, calmly explain that you made a mistake and restate your thoughts in more appropriate language.

In dealing with profanity, most parents find that the more successful they are in ignoring such talk, the more quickly the words disappear. If you feel that you must react, you might remark casually, "We don't use that word. It's a silly way to say . . ." Then say nothing more, carefully ignoring reoccurrences of the language. The worst things you can do are gasp in horror, threaten punishment or laugh if her childlike swearing amuses you. Those are precisely the reactions she is angling for. Do not declare words "naughty"; that is certain to give them special status in your youngster's mind. Neither is it a good idea to be overbearing and press her to define the profanities she utters. That only leads to needlessly complicated explanations.

Sooner or later, you will face the problem of what to do when your youngster cuts loose with a shocker in front of other adults, who may be embarrassed or offended. When that happens, calmly explain that "those are not the kinds of words that we use." Later you may wish to suggest substitute phrasing that is colorful but acceptable and ask your little one to say it that way next time.

Interrupting

Why It Happens

A youngster's natural exuberance, short attention span, single-mindedness and overwhelming desire to express himself all add up to a common childhood failing: He interrupts. The mere sight of you engrossed in conversation, either in person or on the phone, will seem to galvanize your attention-hungry child. Though he may have been tongue-tied a few minutes earlier, now he has a dozen things he wants you to hear or see. You can expect the condition to be at its height when your toddler is learning to talk, but it may continue well beyond school age.

What to Do

Try to anticipate and side-step the problem before it occurs. If you expect visitors or a long phone call when your little one is around, get him started on some activity beforehand. For conversations that you cannot anticipate, keep a busy bag of toys handy for him to dip into; if the toys are used only on such occasions, they may seem more special. In either case, tell the child that you are going to be busy for a little while and that it is his job to play quietly. If you can allow your youngster to be included when you have a visitor, tell him that you and your guest will stop every so often to see how he is getting along. Compliment him on his cooperation each time and ask if he has questions to ask or anything to tell you. If he forgets and interrupts, correct him firmly but pleasantly, in a tone that does not sound like rejection. If he continues to interrupt, you might use a time-out to discipline him; at the same time, ask yourself if perhaps your visit has gone on too long. When the guest has gone, tell your child that you appreciate his efforts.

As always, you have to provide a good model. Try not to allow interruptions when he is involved in a social exchange. If someone calls during storytime, for instance, tell the caller, "I'm sorry but I cannot talk now, we're in the middle of a bedtime story." It is important for children to see that the same rules apply to adults.

Dawdling

Why It Happens

Dawdling is almost certain to occur whenever your youngster faces a task that is boring or disagreeable. And it is often unwittingly reinforced by overworked parents: Always in a rush, they tend to overreact when their youngster responds with the speed of molasses. The youngster thus learns one more way to get a rise out of his parents. But there is another side to dawdling that parents should be aware of: Sometimes what seems like intentional dawdling may not be intentional at all. Until the age of five or six, a child does not have much understanding of time and may not share your concerns about punctuality.

What to Do

Build a reasonably consistent routine into your child's daily schedule. Get him up and dressed at the same hour and arrange meals, play sessions and naps so they consume about the same length of time each day. Gradually, your youngster will absorb a sense of the schedule he is expected to follow. When there are to be special events, alert your child well in advance and begin your preparations far enough ahead that you do not have to rush. Tension only makes a dawdler more uncooperative.

Make boring or repetitive tasks more enjoyable by turning them into racing games, such as a challenge to pick up the toys before a timer rings. Allow enough time for your youngster to succeed in these races. Another approach is to make finishing the task at hand a condition for starting a more pleasant activity: "When you put everything into the box, we can go out for a walk." Praise him as he goes along and be sure to deliver the reward just as soon as the job is done. Above all, do not be a nag; up to a point, it is better to let him dawdle along than to engage in a test of wills. As a subtle prod, you might remind him that he has wasted valuable playtime.

Dressing Problems

Why They Happen

Because parents attach so much importance to how their youngsters look, it is not surprising that dressing often turns into a struggle. Problems generally begin at about two years of age, the underlying issue being one of independence. At that stage, children have begun to assist in dressing themselves but do not have the dexterity to do the whole job and may feel frustrated and a little resentful when you step in to help. A three-year-old may occasionally don garments backward or inside out and be so proud of this triumph that he will resist changing it around. As children grow older, the focus of conflict often shifts to dawdling or to disagreements about what clothes to wear. With the exception of the child who genuinely feels more secure in a particular outfit, all of these problems boil down to a contest to see who is in charge. You will only add fuel to the fire by giving the matter more attention than it deserves or by allowing your child to lure you into no-win arguments.

What to Do

Besides simply keeping your cool, there is much you can do to prevent dressing problems and guide your youngster along the path to good habits. A child typically takes the first step toward dressing by learning to undress. At 18 months, she is proud to show that she can take off her hat and socks or unzip a zipper. By 30 months, she wants to do it all. Encourage her by laying out her clothes on the floor — socks and shoes nearest her feet, pants laid out flat, then the shirt and so on. Stand by to give praise but offer help only when asked. At this stage, do not worry about how long it takes. If you hurry her while she is learning these new skills, they may start to seem onerous and her pace may slow even more.

Provide clothing that is easy to put on: Pants with elasticized waists and pullover shirts with wide neck openings are good choices. Avoid small zippers, buttons and snaps. Buy tube socks that slip on in any direction and help her learn to get her shoes on the right feet by marking red dots on the in-facing sides; all she needs to do is keep the dots together.

By five, most children are capable of getting fully dressed in a reasonable amount of time. They can distinguish fronts from backs, and button most buttons they can see. If your child argues about what she is going to wear, bring her in on the selection process. Limit her choices to clothes that are acceptable to you. Stay calm and simply refuse to argue.

Overall, bear in mind that even well-coordinated six-year-olds may have difficulty with some garments, and that children occasionally revert to helplessness out of a longing for the simplicity of being a baby. However, you also have to be alert for deliberately uncooperative behavior. When a five-year-old suddenly refuses to get dressed or makes intentional mistakes such as reversing her shoes or wearing clothes inside out, treat it lightly. Say: "Aren't you being silly! Now let's see how you do it right." Try to rise above such episodes; otherwise, your youngster is liable to turn a small matter into a major battle.

If the child persists, you can set up contingencies: "When you get dressed, then you can watch cartoons," or, "When you get dressed, you can have breakfast." If the refusal to get dressed continues, try placing your youngster in a time-out. If, after this disciplinary interlude, she still balks at getting dressed, you should repeat the time-out until she decides to comply. Above all, do not leave dressing until the last minute if you are experiencing trouble with it. Have your youngster get dressed as soon as she is up in the morning.

Eating Problems

Why They Happen

Many parents find themselves spending more time and emotional energy on their children's eating habits than on any other aspect of behavior. They worry about the health implications of eating too little, being hungry any time but mealtime or having finicky likes and dislikes. And they fret over such mealtime disturbances as eating in an excessively messy manner, playing with food or being so fidgety that mealtimes become nerve-racking for everyone else.

Your first thought when your youngster refuses to eat or eats very little may be that he is sick. Health problems can occur, of course, but if the change in appetite happens around your child's first birthday, chances are it is merely the body's way of announcing that the growth rate is slowing and that less fuel is needed. Moreover, young children are blessed with an extremely acute sense of taste; coupled with a natural suspicion of new flavors and textures, this sensitivity leads them to reject certain things you would like them to eat. Have a talk with your pediatrician; the doctor will probably reassure you that your toddler's reactions to food are perfectly normal.

Even though eating problems may not be a medical concern, they can still present quite a challenge. Many youngsters discover early in life that there is no more effective means of capturing Mommy's attention — or of demonstrating their independence — than refusing to eat or making a circus of mealtimes. Yet do try to remember that beneath all the stubbornness and lackadaisical dawdling, all the wiggling, spilling, splashing and throwing, your child's skills are progressing on their own timetable, as is his ability to concentrate on what he is doing.

What to Do

If mealtimes are calamities, try isolating the specific problems and working on them one at a time. You will want to begin with a realistic understanding of your child's normal appetite for his age and weight, and adjust your standards and expectations accordingly. Accept the fact that food intake is likely to decrease between the ages of one and two, because of slowed growth and your little one's urgent need to feed himself. Between two and three, his appetite may improve, but now he may develop fussy tastes, with powerful likes and dislikes about what he will eat, and in what order and with what utensils.

His food preferences are likely to become stronger as he gets older, so you should provide him from the start with a diet that has variety and the recommended nutritional balance. But do not become too firmly set on his eating carrots or bananas or any other single item; it usually is easy enough to find food equivalents that he likes.

Keep in mind, too, that your toddler's stomach is best able to handle a limited amount of food at frequent intervals. Serve small portions, so that he has no difficulty finishing what is on his plate; offer more only if he asks. Plan your youngster's eating so that his day includes three regularly scheduled meals — at least one of them with the family, if possible — plus healthy, in-between snacks if he wants them. But do not let snacks take the place of main meals; if he has trouble finishing lunch or supper, you might want to revise his snack schedule or reduce the amount he eats between meals. You should decide when snack-time arrives, of course; he should not eat whenever he wants.

To encourage variety in his diet, you may wish to establish some rules about having to taste specific foods before he can have other foods. While he should taste everything, do not force him to finish things he does not like. You could say, "You can have more potatoes as soon as you taste your beans," or, "You can have dessert, but first taste your carrots." Your best response to confrontations over eating is to withdraw from the battle. The child then discovers for himself that the natural consequence of not eating what is offered, when it is offered, is to go hungry. If a child is otherwise healthy, he should come around to more reasonable eating habits in good time.

Just as you can expect fluctuating appetite levels and food preferences, you can count on the fact that your toddler is going to be a messy eater. His coordination is simply not up to Emily Post manners. As he practices his skills, try to be patient and uncritical. You may need to work on the transition from a high chair to a chair, getting up and down at the table, utensil use or making messes with food. Take up each issue in turn, not all at once. And bear in mind that the days when you are concentrating on skills are not the best times to introduce new foods; instead serve things you know he likes.

Teaching your youngster to sit through a meal can be a challenge all its own. Consider his energy level and estimate how long you can reasonably expect him to sit, then adjust meal periods accordingly. Encourage him by praising his efforts frequently — every one to two minutes, to start — with statements such as: "You've been sitting so quietly and eating so nicely. Mom and I are proud of you when you behave like that." And do not expect your child to sit still and eat while you are up and working around the kitchen; make sure you are sitting also.

You can assist by cutting food into bite-size pieces before meals and by providing eating utensils shaped and scaled to his abilities. Keep the table around him free of extraneous dishes and utensils, so that he has to concern himself only with the essential plate, cup, fork and spoon. An extra-large mat will help contain the mess and give him a sense of place as well.

By the time he is three, your preschooler will probably be fairly adept with his hands. If he still makes a considerable mess, he may just be playing with his food, either to get your attention or simply to amuse himself. Make it clear that this is not acceptable behavior. If he continues, remove his plate for a moment and tell him that the next time you will really have to take away his food; then give him back his plate. Be sure to commend him if he changes his behavior. If he still continues to misbehave, send him away from the table, saying, "I'm sorry you did that. Now your dinner is over."

If your child consistently dawdles or repeatedly refuses to come when he is called to the table, tell him that you are sorry he has missed out on dinner and that you hope he will come when he is called next time. If he arrives with a dirty face and hands, do not serve his food but say, "I see that you are not ready to eat." If he manages to return clean, serve him then, but take his plate away when the rest of the family finishes, whether he has finished or not.

In each of these contests, be friendly, noncombative and

matter-of-fact. Make it clear to your child that you have firm, consistent rules, and that if he insists on doing things his way, he must be responsible for the consequences. Do not become visibly upset, bribe or beg; do not offer substitute foods or substitute mealtimes. And do not give in. Above all, try to keep mealtime pleasant and pay lots of attention to good behavior.

Special Concerns

Overeating is rarely a problem among preschoolers but should not be taken lightly when it occurs. Obesity can do long-term damage to a child's health and self-esteem. Experts suggest that parents of an overeater look to see whether the child is using food as a source of comfort or to calm himself down when he is feeling restless. Try to determine what situations lead to overeating. When during the day does it happen? Structure the youngster's activities so that he has plenty of social and physical stimulation during these periods.

Overeating frequently results when a child simply loves to eat and his parents fail to set limits on snacking. Some parents unwittingly train their children to be problem eaters by giving in quickly to demands for snacks as a way of avoiding tantrums or other disruptive behavior. Whatever its origins, overeating should be handled by limiting the child's access to foods he should not have. One good strategy is to place a special tray in the refrigerator for him with cut-up fruits or other foods that will enable you to control the calories and nutrition.

The seriously overweight child may be experiencing problems other than those mentioned above. If you cannot steer your youngster into more normal eating habits, you probably ought to consult a professional. The condition almost certainly has a physical or emotional base that needs attention.

Bedtime Problems

Why They Happen

Slumbertime can be the most exasperating time of all for many parents. Your youngster may resist going to bed and falling asleep for any number of reasons. He may stay awake out of reluctance to miss what he perceives to be the fascinating activities that go on while he is asleep. Or he may be too excited to go to sleep right away, particularly if he has just finished playing vigorously, or if he has been scolded and is brooding about it. He may simply be one of those children who need to wind down by playing in bed before dozing off. Another possibility is that he may not be sufficiently tired, having had too little exercise or too long a nap. Perhaps he has a certain bedtime ritual that he relies on for reassurance before closing his eyes — and you may have overlooked some important part of the routine. Or he may be an unwilling sleeper because of nighttime fears — fear of the dark, fear of imaginary creatures, fear of having bad dreams, fear of not waking up. Such worries may leave him unable to relax and get to sleep.

Some of these problems are temporary and quickly resolve themselves. Childhood fears, for example, are common between the ages of three and five, but usually wane after that. Those concerns that persist may have a genuine basis in the child's temperament, or they may linger because you have inadvertently allowed yourself to become part of the problem. Parents do this chiefly by responding to a child's bedtime misbehavior in ways that encourage the youngster to continue it.

What to Do

As with almost all behavior problems, the first step is to make certain that you — not your little one — are in control of the situation. Do not wait for overt signs of sleepiness before informing your youngster that it is time for bed. He may be able to get by on quite a bit less sleep than he really needs, but his behavior and your peace of mind will suffer for it. Establish an appropriate bedtime hour according to the child's age and apparent needs. A toddler generally does best on about 12 hours of sleep a night until the age of four, when 11 or 11 and a half hours' sleep a night is adequate. Your youngster will most likely give up his morning nap at around two years of age but may continue his afternoon nap until the age of three or older. The length of the nap starts with a maximum of two hours and gradually tapers off to periods of waking rest. Even at six years of age, most children benefit from an hour of afternoon quiet time

during which they do nothing more strenuous than read. But remember that some two-year-olds do just fine on nine to 10 hours a night, while others profit from 13 hours a night with a couple of hours of naptime for good measure.

Make bedtime routines as predictable as possible. Preschoolers are comforted and relaxed by a familiar pattern at the close of their day. While you will want to keep the routine relatively simple, you should allow plenty of time to go through all the details. Start at least 45 minutes before you want your youngster asleep; that way, even with some dawdling, he can still be in dreamland by the appointed hour. Begin the bedtime preparations by giving him fair warning to finish up whatever he is doing. Some parents find it helpful to alert their youngsters by setting a "first notice" timer for five minutes or so.

When the warning time is up, have your youngster go directly and without bargaining to take his bath, put on his pajamas, brush his teeth, go to the toilet and perform whatever other bedtime chores you have set. To minimize the opportunities for distraction, have him perform the actions in the same order every time. Even so, you will doubtless have to remind the child to stick to business — except for that time in the bath set aside for having fun.

End the routine with a shared activity that your youngster enjoys. A bedtime story is always a good choice, but songs or a back-rub can also be things that he will look forward to. If the child has dawdled excessively getting ready for bed, explain to him that you now have to shorten the treat: Choose a short story rather than a long one or sing one song rather than three. You should not omit the treat altogether, or you will end the day on a tearful and unhappy note.

Let your good-night kiss be the formal signal that the day is over and promptly leave the room. Do not be sweet-talked into answering questions or meeting additional requests unless they are obviously urgent, such as when your toddler is clearly about to wet his bed. If you make exceptions to the parting routine, your quick-witted youngster will soon learn to bedevil you with diversionary tactics every night.

If, despite everything, your child still has difficulty settling down, consider whether his naptime should be reduced, moved to an earlier part of the afternoon or ended altogether. Also try lowering his activity level earlier in the evening. Exciting TV shows right before bedtime are probably not a good idea. And naturally, you should keep down the household noise once the youngster is in bed. Some parents find that quiet music, a humming air conditioner, a whirring fan or some other monotonous sound in the child's room is an effective way of screening out household noises.

Climbing down from bed after lights-out is something most children try from time to time. The ruses are many, various and frequently charming: a glass of water; another trip to the toilet; a sudden pain; something very important to say; a last hug, kiss and "I love you, Mommy." Being a caring — not to say doting — parent, you will find it difficult to resist these ploys. One way to succeed is to make certain that all your youngster's real needs are taken care of during the bedtime routine. Then hold firm. Make the rule about lights-out very precise: no talking, no getting up again, no requests for water or extra bed toys. Just a definitive "good night."

If your toddler repeatedly gets up and comes looking for you, take him calmly by the hand and put him back in bed, without comment or scolding. Do it in a manner that produces a minimum of the attention he is seeking. You may find that you have to repeat this procedure a dozen times or more each night for a few nights. But stick with it. He will soon tire of any trick that does not work. In some cases, you can eliminate the excuse for getting up; if he complains about being thirsty, leave a small glass of water by his bed so he can have a sip when he wants.

Sometimes a toddler will manipulate his parents into keeping him company until he falls asleep, or he will wake at night and crawl into their bed. Your youngster may say he is frightened or not give any reason at all. Unless you are willing to have it become a cast-iron habit, you will have to deal with it quickly and teach him to fall asleep alone. There are various methods, but perhaps the surest is to do it cold turkey, simply letting the child cry himself to sleep — hard as that may be. If you opt for this approach, perhaps you can make it less painful for your youngster by assuring him that you will be close by, even though you are in another room, and that he will see you again first thing in the morning. But do not relent in your insistence that he go to sleep alone.

If your toddler is younger than two years old, you may wish to take a less rigid route. Kiss him good night, then wait outside the door and look in frequently — every 45 to 60 seconds at first — to remind him that "it's night-night now." Do not make eye contact when you reappear. Gradually lengthen the intervals until he finally drops off to sleep: Either approach should succeed in three to five days.

If your little one wakens with bad dreams, be solicitous and comforting, but insist that he remain in his own bed. Staying in his bed reinforces the idea that there really is nothing to be afraid of. If you wish, you can install a small night light or leave on a light in the hall so he can see it glowing under his door. Another strategy is to give him a new stuffed animal or doll that is endowed with special attributes as a "brave companion" and "protector." One other thing that works for some parents is to perform a formal sweep of the room for anything scary, just before the final good-night kiss. Go through the motions of checking the closet and under the bed but do so in such a way that it is obviously a big joke. You want the child to deal with his fears and, at the same time, learn to laugh at them. With his assistance, pronounce the room absolutely safe for sleeping. If nightmares persist, or if your youngster seems profoundly frightened again and again, it may be time for you to consult your pediatrician.

Disruptive Behavior in Public

Why It Happens

Children misbehave in public for many of the same reasons they misbehave at home; they are tired or bored, or perhaps they want attention. What complicates matters is that their embarrassed parents may be reluctant to do anything immediately about it with "the whole world watching." Naturally, a youngster soon discovers that she can get away with things in public that she would never be permitted to do at home.

What to Do

You can help your youngster cope with public situations by taking care to instruct her beforehand on what to expect and how to behave. Tell her that "shopping means walking beside Mom," or, "You may help me look, but you must not touch things." If your child is inclined to whine and beg for her favorite treats in the supermarket, specify at the start one or two items she can pick out and hold the line there.

Start off with a few short excursions so she can practice appropriate behavior. Later, she can graduate to longer trips, but you should try to avoid long, boring expeditions with your young child in tow.

Prepare for the journey by packing a few toys that will help keep her occupied in a strange new place. Consider the nature of the place you are going to and what you will be doing. If you know that you will be spending time in something that is not interesting to your youngster — an extended conversation with adults perhaps — save one special toy that you can give her as a fresh diversion. Or you might want to bring along a box of raisins or some other food treat to reinforce good behavior in the supermarket.

In explaining how you want your child to behave, be positive in your approach; do not go into all the bad things that could happen. If she does get into mischief, it is probably best to give her one warning before imposing a penalty. Your preschooler is sure to be a little off-stride in a strange place, and she may need to be reminded of what you expect. But once the warning has been given, allow no further infractions. If the misbehavior occurs a second time, do precisely what you said you would do.

Many parents find that time-outs are effective away from home, especially if they have figured out in advance where the time-out is to be held and can take the child there promptly. It can be a corner of the store where she will have to stand for a minute or two with her back to the rest of the people while you stand nearby; however, under no circumstances should you leave her there alone. During the time-out permit no toys, conversation or other distractions.

If friends or relatives are along, they may try to reassure you that your child's behavior does not bother them, but you should not let their well-meaning remarks soften your resolve. Similarly, strangers may offer comments or advice about the situation. The best thing is to put aside your embarrassment and deal with the problem the way you have planned in advance, as if there were no one else around. Let your self-appointed helpers know, as politely as you can, that you really do not need their assistance. The issue is between you and your child; you have set standards that your child has chosen to ignore. You might say something like, "Thank you, but I have a way of dealing with this situation that works for us."

Special Concerns

Misbehavior while riding in the car has the added consequence of distracting the driver and endangering everyone. Explain to your child beforehand what you expect of her while you are on the road. And you should make sure that the youngster is wearing her seat belt — both for safety's sake and to limit the amount of mischief she can get into.

Bossiness

Why It Happens

Bossiness is a natural part of growing up. Your preschooler has been on the receiving end of parental direction for three or four years — literally, a lifetime — and it is perfectly understandable for her to try domineering her peers. The rub, of course, is that her playmates are arriving at the same stage at the same time, and when two assertive children confront each other, the results can be unpleasant. There is also the potential for long-range trouble if your child happens to get stuck in this pattern.

What to Do

Give your child a number of chances to assert herself with her playmates. She may discover on her own that continually bumping noses with others brings more problems than benefits.

But if she persists in being bossy, is bossy to an exaggerated degree or has trouble making friends, it is time for you to step in and help. At the appropriate moment, you might say, "People like it better when you take turns. They get angry when you don't want to share." Your child may respond with denials, but you have given her something to think about; chances are, if you calmly point out her bossiness on subsequent occasions,

Carry a collection of toys in your car; if your child is likely to throw or hit, be sure the toys are not the sort that can become dangerous projectiles. Chatting and singing together are good, positive ways to prevent the restlessness and boredom that can lead to problems. And be sure to praise your little one's good behavior, saying something like, "You're learning to be a wonderful car rider."

If your youngster is determined to be obstreperous, pull over to the side of the road and refuse to continue until she settles down. Make clear that is is not safe to drive while she is raising a ruckus. When all is relatively calm and you are under way again, initiate a pleasant conversation and make no further reference to the misbehavior.

When the children in your car-pool are inclined to fight in the back seat, you might want to institute a system of rewards for a reasonably successful trip. For instance, let them hear a penny clink into a jar whenever they sit quietly for a period of time. Then they can count the tokens at the end of the trip and turn them in for treats.

she will begin to adjust her manner.

Your preschooler may need practice playing with children under circumstances conducive to cooperative ventures. You might invite other children over to make cookies together while you monitor the activity. Emphasize the benefits of cooperation with such comments as, "Isn't it nice when people work together." Intervene if they start to squabble; stress how much more fun they could be having if they were sharing.

Nevertheless, being in charge and asserting oneself are perfectly healthy and legitimate needs, and you do not want to squelch them. A good way to experience the positive feelings of being in charge now and then is through such games as red light-green light, statues and Simon says. In such games, your youngster is entitled to tell others what to do — and the more diabolical her demands the better — but she also knows that her moment of glory is limited.

Teasing

Why It Happens

A youngster may first acquire a taste for teasing with innocent name-calling games. As early as three, she may be tagging playmates or siblings with silly rhyming nicknames or scatological epithets. At this stage, she is doing it primarily to amuse herself and exercise her vocabulary. Later, when she discovers that teasing and name-calling are useful tools and potent ways to convey anger, she may carry the game too far. For one thing, such tactics are almost certain to provoke a reaction. To the very young, names — however silly — seem to carry magical powers. When a toddler is called a dummy, she almost certainly believes it to be true. Consequently, when the name-caller strikes, the victims tend to cry or call for help. Things get exciting, and the name-caller is suddenly the center of attention.

What to Do

The first time your youngster calls another person a bad name, let her know that the word is off limits, and that she may not use it as a way to tease others. If she persists, respond calmly but firmly. Tell her, "I'm sorry that you called your sister a bad name," and give her a brief time-out while you turn your attention to the other child. If the victim complains, agree that name-calling is not nice, but you should move on to some other subject as quickly as possible in order to avoid investing the words with undue significance. After the name-caller's penalty is over and play has resumed, make sure to praise the teaser if her behavior improves. "How nicely the two of you are playing together," you might say. "Doesn't it feel terrific to be such good friends?"

Be careful of your own use of names and tease words. Parents sometimes unwittingly encourage name-calling by overusing pet names they have for their children. These are friendly enough among family members, but your youngster may employ them in other situations — and not necessarily with the same affectionate intent.

Tattling

Why It Happens

Most children try tattling as a way of making themselves look good at the expense of a sibling or a playmate. It usually begins around the age of four or five, when youngsters are developing a pride in their knowledge of the rules and are eager to show grownups how well they have learned them. By simply refusing to play along with tattletales, you can generally persuade your little one to discard this tactic as a form of gaining attention. If he continues, he may be telling you that he wants to be reassured of your love and attention and has found tattling an effective means of doing that.

What to Do

In dealing with tattling, you will want to shape your child's behavior selectively. You do not want him to come running with a tale of woe about every tiny little thing another youngster has said or done; in such cases, it is better for him to work it out on his own among his peers. On the other hand, you certainly want him to come to you when confronted with a situation in which someone could get hurt or something valuable could get broken. Your goal is to help him see the difference between these circumstances and to discourage the former while rewarding the latter.

Explain to him that you are generally not interested in hearing him complain about his playmates. When he comes to you with a story about some minor difference, just say: "I'm sorry that you two aren't getting along, but I think you can work it out together." Such a statement divides responsibility for the conflict between the tattler and the told-upon. When the tattler learns that he gains nothing from his tattling, he will most likely abandon it. At the same time, you should tell him quite specifically that you want him to come to you when things seem dangerous to him — when someone is playing with matches, for example, or climbing up high on a ladder. When your youngster comes to you with such reports, be sure to praise him for his help and his caring.

Avoid setting up situations in which you are tacitly endorsing tattling. Do not ask an older child to tell you when a younger one is doing something that he ought not to do, however practical that might seem. It will encourage the older child to use telling as a weapon to control the younger child. And do not encourage a younger child to come to you when older ones are mean to him. If any serious trouble arises, you can be sure that you will hear about it.

Refusing to Share

Why It Happens

Most young children have great difficulty sharing toys and other property with playmates. One reason is that they have no true concept of ownership. To your toddler, ownership or possession means nothing more than whatever she happens to be holding at the moment; thus, if your two-year-old is unwilling to give up her toys but is quick to grab another child's possessions, she is only doing what comes naturally. Before you can get across the notion of sharing, your youngster first has to understand what it means to own something — to have it for herself, to put it where she wants, to use it when she wants and to get it back again when someone else is done with it. Then gradually, she can be taught to part temporarily with something she owns in order to play for a while with something another child owns.

What to Do

You can lay the foundations for learning about sharing when your child is as young as 18 months. Teach your toddler not to grab things but to say "my turn," while you model the way that grownups share. Honor a two-year-old's desire for sole ownership by treating her belongings with respect. Before a playmate comes to the house, ask your child to help you put away one or two of her favorite toys for safekeeping. Then ask her to find something that she would like to share with the visitor. She may have a hard time following through with this plan, but at least you will have introduced the idea of sharing. If possible, have duplicates of some toys so that the children can play side by side without competition for at least part of the visit. When conflicts arise, help resolve the situation in a calm, nonjudgmental manner by offering an alternative plaything to the one who grabs.

With the beginnings of cooperative play — usually around the age of three — expediency starts to figure in your youngster's training. She discovers that give and take go together, and that the only way to persuade a playmate to surrender a desirable toy is to offer an equally desirable one. Memory also begins to help as she sees that toys she shares usually come back in the end. She also begins to realize that when children come to play, they inevitably want to play with her toys.

Use occasions when you share things with your spouse, with friends or with other members of the family to demonstrate that sharing is not only something everyone does but also something they enjoy. Invent games that revolve around sharing, such as pushing one another around in a wagon. With your help,

the child can begin to view her responsibilities as a form of fun rather than as a duty. Put that lesson into words for your youngster and offer praise when she shares the fun of taking turns in the wagon.

At first, you will need to supervise closely when your youngster is in sharing situations. Establish two basic rules for your child and her playmates: No one is allowed to grab a toy that another child is playing with; but anyone is allowed to pick up a toy that is lying unused on the floor. Inevitably, playmates arrive at the point where there is one toy everyone wants at the same time. That is when a kitchen timer comes in handy: Tell the disputants that they will have to take turns and that the timer will ensure equal time with the toy. If the toy continues to cause disputes, take it out of play for 15 minutes. Then give the playmates another chance to practice sharing before they have completely lost interest in the toy. If there are still problems after this step, you should put the toy away for the day. Do not be surprised if certain toys remain too controversial for use in a group for extended periods of time. Sharing is a developmental skill, and many otherwise well-behaved children do not master it for several years.

Biting

Why It Happens

Biting, or to be more accurate, mouthing, may occur in infancy, when your baby uses her mouth and gums to explore things. Some infants also clamp down hard on their mother's breasts, perhaps to relieve sore gums. But true biting, with a set of sharp little teeth, more typically can become a problem between the ages of 18 and 30 months. At this stage, your youngster has very limited verbal ability and uses biting as a form of communication — no different in her view from pushing, grabbing, kissing or patting — except that it gets your attention a lot more quickly. If the recipient of the bite cries out in pain or alarm, your toddler is likely to regard the ploy as an even greater success.

In general, children resort to biting only under narrow circumstances — when they are very tired or have been playing in close quarters with another child. However, biting may also be a way of dealing with stress, anger or frustration.

What to Do

If your baby bites, the best way to discourage her is to respond with an "ouch" and immediately put her down. Quickly removing yourself from physical contact will generally bring an end to a baby's biting. A toddler, who is ready to learn other methods of communication and other outlets for aggression, should be told in plain language that biting hurts people: She must not do it. If she persists, place her in a brief time-out. It is best not to scold or get angry; simply turn your back on the attacker and comfort the victim. As soon as the biter is quiet and under control, allow her to return and show her positive attention, demonstrating that there are better ways to communicate and be noticed. If you suspect that frustration is the cause of the biting, engage her in some simple activity where she can shine.

Try to pinpoint the events leading up to episodes of biting. Does the youngster bite only at certain times of the day? Perhaps the problem occurs before naps or mealtimes, or only during group activities with other children. Does the biting occur during disputes over toys with other children? Is it a response to a change in routine? If you detect a pattern to the biting, you should try to avoid those situations, if possible. Some parents find it necessary to simplify play times, keeping play groups smaller and play periods shorter. If you sense that one of your child's playmates is particularly stressful for her, because of greater assertiveness, dramatically different developmental skills or simply a very different style of play, find other companions or bring the two together under close supervision only.

One point on which all child-behavior experts seem to agree: No matter how distressed or embarrassed or angry you may become at continued biting, one method of correction that is strongly discouraged is biting back just to teach her a lesson. If this sends any message at all, it is that parents hurt people, too. Moreover, the youngster who bites as an expression of anger is only made angrier still, while the very young child is unlikely to make any mental connection between the hurt she feels and the hurt she has produced.

Your child should cease biting for the most part when she begins to master language and can use words to express herself. This usually occurs around the age of three. If biting continues to be a chronic problem beyond this age despite your attempts to intervene, both the underlying conditions that are upsetting the child and the behavioral expression may need professional attention. The key word is "chronic." It is good to remember that biting in an isolated moment of rage does not necessarily signify a serious problem, even in a four- or five-year-old.

Other Concerns

A bite that breaks the skin can cause infection. If the skin is broken, wash the injury thoroughly with soap and water, then apply a sterile dressing and secure it with adhesive tape. Have a doctor look at the wound.

Physical Aggression

Why It Happens

Fighting, hitting, kicking, pinching, hair pulling and other forms of overt aggression are usually physical expressions of a child's fear, frustration, jealousy, anger or pain. Indeed, physical aggression is the principal way some toddlers have of coping with these feelings. If successful, it produces a gratifying sense of power, and perhaps some material benefit — another child's toy. At the very least, it is sure to bring on the parents, who most likely will rush into the fray — scolding, cajoling and becoming emotionally involved. Naturally, their little brawler gets more attention more quickly than he would have attracted had he behaved amicably.

The presence of siblings complicates the picture. For a time, squabbling may be one of the main modes of interaction between two children in a family. This can be particularly true when siblings are close in age or otherwise powerfully competitive. Often, the stronger and the weaker work together in what might be termed a conspiracy of self-fulfilling prophecies. In this classic scenario, they fight because they are certain that you will respond by punishing the older and coddling the younger, thus proving the older child's contention that you are unfair and confirming the younger child's sense of himself as weak, helpless and victimized. But be forewarned: The dynamics that shape a relationship between siblings may shift back and forth depending on ages and situations; it is often difficult to know just why your youngsters are at each other's throats.

Fighting can begin as early as 15 or 16 months. A toddler does not fight in the purposeful way that an older child does. Rather, he acts without regard for who or what may suffer in the process; and when he strikes out physically, he makes no clear distinction between animate and inanimate objects. By 30 months, however, he has begun to attack other children with the intent to hurt. This is especially true in disputes over toys that he sees as unquestionably his.

For most children, physical aggression is common but transient until the age of three. After that, aggression usually begins to decrease as a youngster develops the language skills to substitute angry words for physical attacks. Yet even then, the arrival of a new baby in the family can set off another round of aggressive behavior. The shift to a more peaceful attitude also may come more slowly if physical violence is prevalent in your home, either because of aggressive older children or your own tendency to mete out harsh physical punishments. These set examples for a child to follow.

Whatever your child's particular circumstances, expect him to be more aggressive any time he is under sustained stress. The sixth year, which coincides with the beginning of formal school, is one of those periods, marked among boys in particular by strong tendencies to fight.

What to Do

You have two objectives in dealing with physical aggression. The first is to intervene immediately when one child threatens the safety of another. Some youngsters will reach for anything handy when fighting. Obviously, if the weapon is heavy or sharp, you have to confiscate it instantly. The second goal is to handle such episodes in a way that discourages aggressive behav-

ior while encouraging other solutions to problems. Try not to show anger, exact stiff punishments or assign guilt or innocence, for in doing so, you give recognition and dignity to the fighting. To a very young child who has become aggressive in pursuit of another child's toy, assign an immediate time-out. If your child and a particular companion tend to fight frequently, the best antidote is simply to keep them away from each other.

When the battlers are siblings, of course, your only option is to help them find ways of getting along. You can begin imposing the responsibility for peaceful coexistence on them as soon as they are skilled enough to settle disputes on their own. Tell them that they must learn to work out their problems in a nice way and that you will not tolerate fighting, hitting or tattling. Make it a rule that when they fail to settle disputes amicably, it is grounds for an immediate time-out, during which they must go to separate rooms to get themselves under control. If a toy is the point of contention, it automatically goes out of circulation for at least 15 minutes — and even longer as the children get older. Be calm and consistent in enforcing these rules. If fights between siblings seem to occur at particular times of day, plan on separate activities during those times. Reward your youngsters with a pleasant activity when they get along cooperatively for a stretch of time; make the reward something that they can look forward to, such as an extra 15 minutes of play before bedtime. And help the children find acceptable ways to express their aggression: Encourage them to talk about negative feelings instead of acting them out, and if necessary, set up a role-playing situation to show how people can solve problems without raising a big fuss.

Destruction of Property

Why It Happens

Few children are deliberately destructive, but even the most well-behaved youngster lacks judgment and is unfamiliar with the way objects are meant to be handled. Inevitably, things wind up broken, scratched, soiled, torn, dismantled or — that specialty of the adventurous young — flushed down the toilet.

The crisis usually occurs as a consequence of some other aspect of a child's behavior, such as her curiosity and need to explore. She may be enticed by a clock with a second hand going around and end up pulling the hands off it. Or she may become frustrated because what she is trying to accomplish is too difficult; bending the pieces of a tricky cardboard puzzle may be easier than putting them together properly.

What to Do

You cannot teach your toddler to refrain from handling objects, but you can prevent a fair amount of damage by planning. Obviously, you should lock up your fragile treasures or otherwise put them out of reach. And you can take a number of steps to childproof her playthings and living area.

Give your one-year-old toys that are strong enough to withstand her manipulation: A play clock with hands that can be moved, a simple xylophone that can be hammered on to produce sounds, toys that stack and blocks of a size suitable for her age are good choices. Provide cloth books for the youngster who cannot yet handle paper books and give her paper that you specifically designate as paper for tearing and cutting.

You also can control her chances to be destructive. Keep the bathroom door closed and accompany her on missions to the toilet. A child who loves to play in water can be offered safe alternatives, such as a plastic dishpan filled with water and assorted containers for pouring and scooping. If she enjoys making messes, give her messy things to play with — sand, play dough or paints — under your supervision. Make sure to put her in old clothes or a smock, and find her a place where she can play as much as she pleases without damaging anything.

Even though she is only a child, your youngster has to live within the normal environment, and she should start learning to respect the things around her at an early age. When your little one grabs your necklace and tries to yank it free, tell her firmly but pleasantly that your necklace is not a toy and say, "No, you may not pull." If she repeats the behavior, and she probably will,

set her down — to let her know you mean business — and repeat the instruction. Then pick her up again and, if she does not grab this time, give her a hug, saying, "Good girl!"

As your child gets older and her verbal understanding increases, continue to tell her clearly what she may and may not handle. And give her gentle instructions and demonstrations of how you expect her to use the toys and tools you permit: "Books are not for tearing; books are for reading. This is the way to turn pages so that they don't tear," or, "This is your very own coloring book. You may use your crayons only in your coloring book." If the destructive behavior stems from a particular activity, such as jumping on beds, for example, find her a permissible outlet for her energy — an old day bed in the playroom, or a child's indoor trampoline, perhaps.

Be quick to intervene when your youngster starts being destructive. Tell her immediately that what she has done is a no-no and explain once again the correct behavior or way to care for the item. If she persists, call time-out, stop the play altogether and take the troublesome item away for a short time; you can let her have it again later in the day. If you feel that the situation requires a punishment other than time-out, take action immediately and in proportion to the misbehavior, such as making her wash her crayon marks off the wall, or pick up all the pieces of paper she has torn and put them in the wastebasket.

Destructiveness can be a result of carelessness. With some children, parts of toys always seem to be missing or mixed up in boxes with other toys; or objects are left where they are sure to get dirty, torn or broken. Try to reinforce the idea that all belongings deserve good care. Provide her with attractive places to keep her things and see that she puts them there when she is not using them. Praise her when she puts things away. Once your youngster develops a sense of ownership, usually around the age of five, careless damage will lessen dramatically.

As for the willfully destructive child, time-outs and reprimands will not by themselves alleviate the problem. Such children need help learning to deal with their emotions, as well. Younger children of two to three can become destructive as part of a temper tantrum; older children who destroy things may feel profoundly frustrated. Try to observe with what objects and under what conditions your youngster tends to become destructive. If she seems bent on ruining the belongings and work of one child in particular, you can suspect that she is expressing jealousy and may need more love and attention.

If, on the other hand, she attacks her own work and her own toys — if she tears up a painting that is half done, or if she knocks down her construction in disgust — she may be telling you that she is frustrated by a sense of failure, or that the toys she has are too difficult for her level of patience and skill. You can ease her frustration by gently showing her how to accomplish what has eluded her: "Here is a way to make the blocks stack up tall," or, "These blocks can't pile any higher, but here is a way to lay them out sideways. See what a fine train they make!"

As your youngster gets older, talk about how to deal with frustration well before she reaches the point of destructiveness. Find neutral times to discuss good and bad ways to express feelings. Help her understand that it is all right to feel angry and frustrated, but that you want to help her find better ways to express those feelings than by breaking things. And finally, as you work to help her control her behavior, avoid nagging or scolding, which only intensifies her negative feelings.

Throwing Objects

Why It Happens:

Throwing things is unquestionably fun. Many a youngster starts throwing things simply to express himself physically when he is less than a year old, deliberately tossing the same rattle on the floor again and again to watch Mom fetch. But as your child grows older, throwing can turn into an expression of anger and frustration, particularly if he has not learned any alternative means of venting his negative feelings. And as play moves from plastic rattles to wooden blocks and his hand-eye coordination improves, his aim can become dangerously accurate, making this mode of attack against playmates, pets and parents all the more enticing.

What to Do

From the start, discourage deliberate throwing, as distinct from the clumsy or absent-minded dropping of things. Many babies make a game of throwing things on the floor for Mommy and Daddy to pick up, which may delight the parents as well as the child — for the first few rounds. When the novelty wears off and you wish to bring this sport to an end, pick the item up and return it once or twice with a firm, "That's all," or, "No more throwing." If he persists after that, lay the object aside until another time when he may be more inclined to hold onto it. Be prepared to withstand his protests and praise him when he plays properly with things.

If, as your child gets older, he continues to throw things, aiming to hit someone, intervene immediately and tell him, "Time-out. No throwing. You are not allowed to hurt other children." Then review the action, showing him the correct response: "Joshua made you angry when he took the toy. Tell him you want to play with the toy. Let's take turns. Joshua can play with it now. Then it will be your turn." When your child hears these model ways of dealing with conflicts enough times, he will start to use them instead of acting out his feelings of anger. You might also try role playing, with you in the role of another child and your youngster as the one who must find a friendly way to share his toy. Praise his suggestions and lead him subtly in the acceptable directions.

At the same time, show your child that there are right times and places to throw things, and that skill in this kind of throwing earns praise. Children as young as 18 months can begin to play a tossing game with a foam-rubber ball and a wastebasket. Five- and six-year-olds may enjoy an outdoor sport called pebble toss, in which they compete with each other to hit a tin can a few feet away. Make the rules simple but explicit: both children safely behind the throwing line, taking turns and using pebbles of a certain size. Monitor the game until you feel sure that both children can be relied on to play safely. And praise them for playing the game so well.

Lying

Why It Happens

Young children often play fast and loose with what adults consider the truth, yet this does not mean that they are consciously lying. Children up to the age of six see the world largely as it affects them. If they are stretching the truth or telling a falsehood, it is usually because they think what they are saying is right or will bring about positive results.

A child younger than four may exaggerate or misdescribe what she has experienced simply because she still has only rudimentary skills in remembering details and organizing her experiences. For Susie, the most important fact about an event may be that "Janie hit me," not that she provoked Janie by calling her a name.

Even among four- and five-year-olds, this kind of "lying" is usually without malicious intent. Still experimenting with language and social skills, preschoolers lie because they are learning that what they say can determine what will happen. Your youngster might think, If I say I haven't had a cookie yet, then Mommy will give me another one. Between four and six, lying is often self-protective. A child might think, If I say I didn't break the lamp, then I won't have to go to time-out.

Since preschoolers do not understand subtle differences in lying, they seldom tell white lies. In fact, young children are more likely to be embarrassingly blunt in situations calling for tact. "Why are you wearing such an ugly dress?" is a much more realistic response from a young child than a forced, "Yes, I think your dress is pretty."

What to Do

In teaching your youngster not to lie, you should start by getting across the idea that telling the truth is important and that lying has unpleasant consequences. Your child must come to understand the concept of trust and that it is to everyone's benefit for her to be truthful. You might say to her: "I like it when you tell me exactly what happened because then I know I can trust you."

Encourage your youngster to talk openly with you about what is going on in her life. Remember that she will tell you her version of reality, and help her see what is truthful about the event she is describing and what is not. You will probably have to draw the stories out and fill in some blanks for her. The child who says, "Janie hit me," is concerned only with this fact. To get at the whole picture, you will need to engage her in a discussion: "That must have made you very sad. Was it because you called Janie a name?" Eventually, she will begin to understand what really happened and review an event more freely in her own mind.

In all cases, how you handle the questioning will determine whether you encourage truthtelling or fabrication. Do not ask her if she did something when you already know that she did; this only gives her the opportunity to lie in hopes of avoiding punishment. Instead, say: "I know you broke the vase"; then wait for her response. If she admits it, say: "I'm glad you told me the truth. But you know the rule about not throwing balls in the house. For breaking that rule, you get a time-out, but since you told me the truth, it will be only a short time-out." In this way, you are praising honesty while remaining firm about the rules.

If your youngster insists that she is innocent and you know otherwise, you will have to punish her for lying also. Tell her: "You will have to go to time-out for playing ball in the house, and since you did not tell me the truth, you cannot watch your cartoon show on TV this afternoon." This will make it clear that lying leads to doubly unpleasant consequences.

If you did not actually see your child misbehave, and she denies doing it, you should accept her word, while letting her know that you are skeptical: "I hope you're telling me the truth, because if you're not, it will make me very sad." Then drop it; you cannot punish what you did not see.

Cheating

Why It Happens

Cheating is a predictable consequence of introducing young children to games and sports at a time when they can understand the rewards of winning but not the strictures against breaking rules or being dishonest. As your young and inexperienced player sees himself outclassed in many situations, he is likely to change the rules in his favor or to cheat outright in order to win. His self-centered view of life makes it hard to put things in perspective, and winning becomes the most important thing at that moment. By the time he is six, he may have developed far enough intellectually and ethically to be intolerant of cheating in others, but he probably will not be consistent in applying the same standards to himself.

What to Do

Introduce your four- and five-year-old to games and other competitive activities gently and by stages. Set aside time regularly to play simple board games and put the emphasis on the fun rather than on the competitive outcome. Simplify the rules to help him stay within them. Gently suggest a move now and then, so that he wins at least half the time in the beginning. If he loses too often, he may lose his self-confidence as well as the game.

Treat cheating as something that spoils the game rather than something your youngster should be deeply ashamed of. You might want to supervise new games with playmates, taking the role of good-humored referee. If your child or anyone else needs to be corrected, you should do so with a minimum of fuss, so that the youngster is not humiliated before his peers.

If by six, your child still cheats frequently, then you might examine what he has learned about competition. Do you set excessively high standards? Do you praise him only for winning and treat losing as a form of personal failure? If so, your youngster might fall back on cheating as a solution to the bind you have put him in.

Stealing

Why It Happens

Like "lying," the term "stealing" can properly be applied only to those who are old enough to have a fully developed conscience and a clear sense of ownership. These are seldom seen in a child younger than six years of age. The preschooler who takes the belongings of another may be acting out of a number of different motives, but stealing, which means willfully and knowingly taking the belongings of another, is almost certainly not one of them.

Your two-year-old starts from the premise that everything in the world is potentially hers; when she takes some desirable toy from another child, she has no difficulty seeing herself as the rightful owner. At three, she still does not understand the limits of ownership; she retains the notion that she can take things any time she wants. It will be another year before she has developed sufficiently to grasp the idea of ownership, and she will be six before she is really able to see that taking things without permission is unacceptable.

What to Do

You must be prepared to intervene calmly and firmly when your youngster takes things that are not hers, while teaching other ways of dealing with her desires. Start demonstrating the basic rules of ownership by using such words as "mine" and "yours." Frequently remind her that "you must not take something that is not yours," or that "taking things you have not paid for is wrong." When your youngster does take something improperly, accompany her to the store or to the friend's house and have her return the item herself. If the problem continues, you should show her the serious consequences by withdrawing a privilege she holds dear.

Remember not to label the infractions with heavy words such as "steal" and "thief." Such terms are not only inaccurate descriptions of what happened, but they are liable to haunt her later when she realizes how seriously society regards such behavior. If your child denies having taken something, but you are suspicious, do not hesitate to search her or her room in a matter-of-fact way. If you are convinced that she has taken something, confront her directly: "I know you took something that doesn't belong to you."

Avoid putting too strong an emphasis on what your child must not do. Put just as much energy into educating her in the right ways to get what she wants. Talk to her about how you buy things at the grocery store and borrow books at the library, and go out of your way to ask your youngster for permission to use her special cup. She will get the idea.

4 Getting Along with Others

As children grow out of the ego-centered stages of earliest childhood and become more attuned to the world around them, they increasingly enjoy one another's company. The leaf-tossing pair pictured at right demonstrate the sheer delight that little ones take in unabandoned play with each other. But youngsters at play are actually engaged in the very important business of learning to get along with people. Indeed, the social skills involved in making and keeping friends are among the most important abilities a child will ever acquire. Not only do they contribute to his pleasure and emotional well-being in childhood, but also, as long-term studies have shown, children who learn to get along with their peers early in life have fewer problems later on.

Every child is different, of course, and while one youngster may be perfectly happy with only one or two close friends, another will not be satisfied until he has assembled a whole band of companions. As a parent, you should play the role of facilitator rather than director of your child's social life. He may need a fair amount of supervision when he is very small; but from the preschool years on, chances are he will be able to socialize on his own as long as you provide opportunities for associating regularly with other children. Should he encounter an occasional stumbling block, it is all right to step in with a tactful suggestion or to teach him some alternate ways to behave around others. Just make sure to respect his individual temperament and preferences in doing so — and avoid trying to make a quiet, reflective child into a social butterfly, or vice versa.

One of the best ways to ensure that your child will be at ease in a world of peers is for you to establish a warm and loving relationship with him — the wellspring of all subsequent socialization. Then, as he meets other youngsters and establishes new ties, your child will have a solid starter set of social skills to carry with him into the world beyond the family circle.

What Children Gain from Their Peers

Although the early parent-child bond lays the groundwork for later social adjustment, your child probably will learn as much about the practical aspects of being sociable from other youngsters as she will from you. Through her relations with her fellows, she discovers the great diversity of the human race — and finds ways to get along with different types of people.

A world of equals

Your child's interaction with other youngsters — unlike her relationship with you — is rooted in equality. Peers have similar developmental abilities and needs, and they expect to partake of the same social rights and privileges. The situation is quite different between parent and child. From a parent, a child requires nurturing and discipline, security and love. And, while parents are deeply attached to their offspring, they do not depend on them as children depend on their parents.

The fact, then, that parents and children are not social equals — as well as the deep attachment between them — puts a crimp in the child's freedom to engage in various types of social behavior. With peers, a youngster is free to test opinions, to argue or to experiment with aggressive conduct without fear of serious consequences. It is often difficult for a child to try such renegade behaviors with a parent, whose love and approval are vitally important. Finally, when things are not working out between herself and a playmate, the child can simply walk away. Unlike family bonds, peer relationships are voluntary.

How children teach each other

The feedback that children give other boys and girls about their conduct is one important way they educate one another. A youngster who warmly accepts the friendly overtures of playmates, for example, is showing them that they are on the right track with their open, pleasant behavior.

Peers also model behavior for one another, much as a parent does for a child. Thus, by watching and imitating another child — as he asserts himself in a game of tag, for example — a youngster expands her repertoire of mannerisms and actions.

Social skills and attitudes

One of the most fundamental social skills children develop in their play with others is the ability to communicate. Since a toddler cannot count on a fellow toddler to translate his babyish codes, as his parents can do, he must make more of an effort to articulate his thoughts. Similarly, the child learns how to assert himself in order to engage other youngsters in activities.

Youngsters give each other lessons in aggressive behavior and in stereotyped sex roles, too. While these lessons often trouble

A trio of preschoolers play in a shallow parkland stream and chat, perhaps pretending to be fishing. Their harmonious interaction shows that they have mastered the important skills of communicating, cooperating and coordinating activities.

parents, in most cases they do no lasting harm and actually provide valuable information. Aggression is something the child will encounter in one form or another throughout his life. By exploring it in early childhood with youngsters his own age, he learns how to handle his own combative feelings — and how to take care of himself when others challenge him. Eventually, he also sees which aggressive acts are hurtful and distasteful — to others as well as to himself — and moderates his conduct accordingly.

Stereotypes of sex roles are generally acquired first at home, then played out with peers. Young children hold firm views about appropriate behavior for each sex and may ignore or criticize youngsters who engage in play that goes against convention. Even when such behavior conflicts with what you teach your child, it is healthy for him to find out what others think.

The progress of peer relations

Perhaps the most important lesson children learn from one another is how to coordinate their play and cooperate, meshing individual desires with group needs. Learning to share, to take turns and to resolve conflicts amicably is a gradual process that extends throughout the toddler and preschool years — and beyond. The chart on the following eight pages traces the normal stages of socialization that children go through in the first six years of life. ❖

Milestones of Social Development

Birth to 12 Months

Parents dominate the baby's social life during the first months. In fact, it is the mutual love that develops between parents and infant during this period that sets the stage for future relationships, providing the youngster with the sense of security and trust in others that he needs in order to form ties to his peers. While infants do not actually play with each other, they do show considerable interest in other babies and sometimes react to what another child is doing; for example, one infant may cry when he hears another's screams. Toward the end of the first year, a child may start to imitate a peer's actions or play alongside him, as the two babies shown below are doing. The pair, however, probably will not interact in any sustained fashion.

Peer Interaction

Play Behavior

General Social Behavior

- During the first month, the infant has little contact with peers but spends time adjusting to his body, his surroundings and his parents.

- By two months, a baby may look at another infant who is crying or physically active. In another month, he will reach out to touch the baby and, by six months, may direct a smile at him. Older babies explore each other's mouths, eyes and ears as if they were fascinating objects.

- An infant also will pay attention to another baby who is playing with an interesting toy. For example, an eight-month-old may crawl over to a baby who is holding a stuffed animal and attempt to take it away.

- The baby's ability to play, both by himself and with others, increases steadily throughout the first year, and he is able to concentrate on a toy or an activity for longer and longer periods of time. Much of the child's play, especially during the early months of life, is solitary.

- At about four months, the baby will begin to laugh out loud when you include him in an activity.

- After the first few months, the baby explores objects and people intently — with eyes, hands and mouth. The child also likes to test for a response — by shaking a rattle, for example, or dropping a ball.

- The eight- to 12-month-old baby enjoys repetitive games such as peekaboo and pat-a-cake.

- Toward the end of this year, the baby will copy simple actions. If you clap your hands, for example, or make clucking noises with your tongue, he will try to imitate you.

- The newborn knows how to get attention primarily with cries. By two months of age, however, the infant will smile and babble to keep another person's attention and will turn away to break contact.

- When a young baby is troubled, a physical touch, a quiet voice or a comforting face will often soothe him.

- An infant watches people intently, concentrating on their faces. After the first two months of life, he recognizes his parents by sight, smell and the sound of their voices.

- Throughout the first half of the year, the baby becomes progressively more extroverted, reaching out to people with smiles and babbling. A baby will develop preferences for particular people, such as family members and a regular caregiver, between three and six months of age.

- The baby's attachment to his parents is firmly established by the end of the first year. At about eight months, he may begin to demonstrate some signs of anxiety about strangers, becoming less responsive to unfamiliar people. Many babies of this age show their wariness by crying or frowning when approached by people they do not know.

- By about eight months, the baby will perform for familiar people, repeating actions for which he has received attention.

12 Months to Two and a Half Years

During this year-and-a-half stretch the baby becomes a toddler, and peer relationships blossom as the child begins to identify with his peers, apparently recognizing them as his physical and emotional equals. A one-year-old is just becoming aware that another baby, unlike an object, will respond to his behavior and initiate stunts of his own. In contrast, by two and a half, toddlers are actively playing with each other — beginning to take turns, imitating each other's actions and even sharing in a rudimentary way at times. The youngster's emerging language skills help him communicate as he plays; and older toddlers may undertake ambitious enterprises, as the pair shown below is doing by building a tower from blocks. At this stage, play most often revolves around toys and objects. Nonetheless, the cooperation is an impressive accomplishment, requiring toddlers to coordinate desires, plans and activities — no small feat for two little people who are only now learning to talk.

Peer Interaction

Play Behavior

General Social Behavior

- The child's overtures to peers become more mature. A one-year-old might start an exchange by looking at another baby's face while touching it. A few months later, to initiate contact, the child will extend an object, babble and laugh.

- Interaction between peers begins to include give and take and reciprocal role playing. Children of this age will imitate each other and coordinate play actions. One child will first chase his playmate around the room, for example; then the two will switch roles and the playmate will do the chasing.

- While an infant tends to approach another baby with a serious or neutral expression on his face, a toddler will smile and laugh, revealing pleasure as well as interest.

- Though generally friendly, a youngster at this stage can also become angry and aggressive, grabbing toys, refusing to share or screaming when another child takes a toy from him.

- If another child is receiving attention from an adult, the toddler may try to divert attention to himself.

- Children this age will show a preference for one child over another, seeking playmates with similar skills, temperament and behavior. A physically active toddler will usually gravitate toward an energetic acquaintance; a quiet child is more apt to establish bonds with another toddler like himself. The toddler also will distinguish between a familiar and an unfamiliar peer, usually preferring the familiar child.

- Play between toddlers most often centers on objects. A toddler frequently will initiate contact by offering a toy to another child, for example, and then may attempt to use it jointly with his new playmate. Or children may play alongside each other with similar toys.

- Although toys facilitate play between peers, toddlers will be drawn to each other even when no toys are available, often interacting more directly in such situations than when an object is the center of their attention.

- Most social play takes place with only one other toddler. The child also enjoys playing by himself and will engage in soli-tary activities, such as hammering pegs into a workbench and leafing through picture books.

- While a toddler enjoys a vigorous romp with his parents, he may turn more often to peers — when they are present — for play involving toys or physical activity.

- A toddler readily shows love for his parents, offering kisses and hugs without being prompted.

- A natural ham, the child this age appreciates being the center of attention, and if you give your approval to his antics, he will carry them further. He has a sense of humor and will laugh at your capers and his own. He also delights in surprises.

- The child's urge for independence is strong at this stage, but so is his need to feel securely attached to his parents. The two conflicting feelings often compete with each other for control of the toddler's conduct: He may boldly greet an acquaintance one moment, then return to cling to your side the next. And he is frequently shy with unfamiliar adults.

- During this year-and-a-half period, the child may be more interested in and comfortable with peers than with adults he does not know. Peers seem to offer him reassurance in new surroundings and situations.

Two and a Half to Four Years

The child leaves much of her babyish social behavior behind over the course of these 18 months. Peers are increasingly important, and she becomes more actively involved in her activities with them than before. She is more apt to share toys and take turns now, although she still may need some parental encouragement to do so.

Language skills have improved to the point that two children playing together can chat easily about what they are doing, expressing opinions and making plans that keep the activity going. The pair of budding artists in the picture below, for example, are doing more than simply painting alongside each other, as they might have done as toddlers. Instead, the child on the left is commenting about her friend's painting — probably offering a well-meant suggestion.

Children also increasingly enjoy imaginary play during this period. At first, pretend play with peers often involves some version of playing house, as does solitary activity. When playing by herself, the child may conduct an imaginary tea party attended by dolls, or perhaps by invisible acquaintances.

Peer Interaction

Play Behavior

General Social Behavior

- The child's drive to establish relationships with her peers grows stronger during this year and a half. She needs little encouragement to play with other children, as long as you provide the opportunities — by enrolling her in nursery school or a play group, or by inviting other children to play in your home and supplying toys and materials.

- In their interactions, children talk, smile, laugh and engage in rough-and-tumble activities more and more; conversely, they less frequently exhibit such babyish mannerisms as staring and crying in the presence of peers.

- Children of this age start to reinforce each other's social behavior, offering attention and affection to playmates. Young-sters who offer friendship freely find themselves at the receiving end more often than shyer children.

- As they move into the preschool years, children become more aggressive with each other, quarreling over possessions more often than over anything else. Some youngsters become bossy at this stage, exhibiting a desire to control or direct the actions of playmates.

- Around the age of four, feelings of competition and rivalry may emerge, serving as incentives for children to perform tasks well. However, despite their aggressive and competitive behavior, the general tone of peer relations is increasingly one of friendliness and cooperation.

- While peer play in these months most often involves just two children, a preschooler will play in a small group more frequently than she did as a toddler. Once bonds form among youngsters, the group may resist the introduction of a new-comer. But at this stage friendships shift rapidly, and a child who is excluded one day may be warmly welcomed the next.

- With adult supervision, children of this age enjoy playing in larger groups, too. They like to dance, play musical instruments and participate in games such as ring-around-a-rosy.

- In general, children cooperate with each other more often in their play now, especially toward the end of the period. They agree on division of labor in their activities, for example, and are able to give group concerns precedence over their own individual desires.

- Preschoolers play more often with peers of the same sex than with those of the opposite sex. By the age of three, children have definite ideas about activities that are appropriate for each sex and often avoid playing with children who do not conform to their views. For example, playmates may ignore a girl who plays with trucks or a boy who plays with dolls.

- During this year and a half, most youngsters become more and more engaged in imaginary play. Typically, early pre-schoolers take on various family roles and act out scenes they have observed at home.

- Although the child enjoys being with her parents, she is becoming less dependent on them for constant support. In familiar surroundings, most children willingly leave their parents and involve themselves in separate activities.

- As she grows out of toddlerhood and into the preschool stage, the child enjoys helping around the house and finds doing things for others satisfying.

- More capable of making decisions on their own now, children of this age often like to give orders and may delight in switching roles with Mommy or Daddy, just for the fun of it.

- A preschooler will show affection to adults as well as to children, but the youngster begins to look to her peers as well as to adults for attention.

- Frequently, a preschooler will become devoted to the parent of the opposite sex, making declarations of love and expressing a desire to marry the parent.

- An imaginary friend may appear in the child's life. This companion may be invisible or may be a stuffed animal or doll that the child treats as a living creature. Having such imaginary playmates often serves as a way for the child to work out any fears or confusions she may have.

Four to Six Years

A child sharpens her social abilities during this period, learning to get along with peers better than in previous years and taking the initiative in selecting her playmates. This is the result of development in a number of areas: Her communication skills are much improved, for instance, and she has had several years of practice playing with other youngsters. With greater emotional maturity, she can also better control her impulses and delay gratification of her needs. Consequently, the child can coordinate her activities with one or two other preschoolers relatively well, which means that she is able to play for longer periods of time with peers, and that conflicts and quarrels with others are less frequent.

Toward the end of these two years, youngsters may play simple board games in small groups, as the children pictured below are doing. Such games require sophisticated communication abilities as well as an interest in directly competing in contests and skilled tasks — a trait that is only beginning to emerge in most children as the preschool years draw to a close.

Peer Interaction

Play Behavior

General Social Behavior

- As the child moves toward school age, she increasingly seeks attention from peers rather than trying to obtain affection from adults. She may do this by offering a toy to a friend, by suggesting a joint activity or by volunteering her name in introduction to someone she does not know.

- By the age of five or six, the child is actively choosing her own friends rather than agreeing to play with whoever is nearby. Although even babies express preferences for people, it is not until these years that youngsters regularly exercise choice in playmates. Typically, a child who is asked to explain why she is friends with another preschooler will say that she likes the person — or the person likes her — and that she and her friend enjoy some of the same activities.

- Aggression between children remains strong during the course of these two years, but youngsters handle their conflicts somewhat differently now. Older preschoolers will often express their differences verbally as well as physically, in contrast to the purely physical skirmishes of the earlier years. As their use of language improves, there will be increasingly more arguments and fewer fisticuffs.

- Children of this age are increasingly successful at working together to solve simple problems, such as how to balance a box atop a column of blocks. This development is largely due to their better communication skills and the cooperative spirit that accompanies their growing emotional maturity.

- Peer play at this stage generally involves two or three children, although youngsters occasionally form larger groups. Boys tend to play with a wider circle of friends of the same sex than girls; girls' relationships are generally more intense than those of boys.

- At five or six, the child's pretend play becomes more detailed, adhering more closely to reality. Children now will act out scenes with close attention to the way they actually occur, and they often incorporate real-life events into their dramatic play and fantasy constructions.

- Older preschoolers enjoy playing together outdoors with a fair degree of independence. Because they can understand and obey rules better at this stage, they can play with less supervision than in previous years.

- Boys tend toward physically active games; girls are likely to engage in more dramatic and artistic activities — dress-up and painting, for instance. When girls and boys play together, however, they do not engage in such highly stereotyped activities, instead choosing more neutral pursuits such as table games and building blocks.

- Play becomes smoother, with more give and take. Youngsters are able to make decisions about how to conduct an activity and agree on what constitutes fair play. This helps sustain their play for a longer time than in earlier years.

- Children of this age have firm attachments to home and family, coupled with a strong drive to make friends.

- Older preschoolers are acquiring courteous expressions such as "please" and "thank you" and will use them in some social situations, although there will be many lapses.

- Interest in sex differences and in how babies are made and born is high during this period. Playing doctor with a friend is one way a child explores differences and attempts to satisfy her natural curiosity.

- Children of this age are generally enthusiastic about life and show a willingness to try new things — qualities that contribute to a high potential for sociability as youngsters prepare to venture into the world of elementary school and take on the new challenges that await them there.

The Multiple Ingredients of Friendship

Although a child's sociability naturally improves with age, getting along with other young children requires any number of specific interpersonal skills — some taught by parents, others gained through the child's own experience. Through observing children at play, experts have identified several broad categories in which children become socially adept with peers. First, a youngster must learn to approach other children in a manner that encourages a positive response. A variety of interaction skills — such as sharing and respecting the wishes of playmates — are required to keep a social exchange going for any length of time. And finally, the ability to resolve conflicts is a third major social feat that young children must master.

To practice such skills, a youngster needs plenty of trial-and-error encounters with other boys and girls — at home, on outings, at nursery school or in a play group. But keep in mind that children also learn friendship skills by watching their parents. If you demonstrate warm, cooperative behavior in your own friendships, you will be giving your child a constructive model. Your personal style with your child is important, too: A youngster whose parents are attentive and supportive very likely will approach playmates with the same happy attitude.

Approaching other children

Children encounter two distinct situations calling for skill in initiating contact with peers, each with its own particular requirements. In the first instance, a child may want to play with one other youngster. Here, a direct greeting often breaks the ice very nicely. A two-year-old might hold out a toy to another toddler; a four-year-old might introduce herself and ask the other child to play. At either age, if the children agree on an activity, they probably will begin to play together.

Breaking into a group of youngsters busily playing, on the other hand, calls for much more subtlety. Among children, a loose coalition can quickly become an exclusive club with esoteric membership requirements. Consequently, a child who seeks to join such a group must resort to indirect maneuvers, rather than barging in all at once. A tactic known as hovering — which children who are socially adept seem to employ as a matter of course — is among the most effective. For example, a child at nursery school who thinks it might be

Saying goodby to a friend, a small girl assists her friend into a jacket. Helpful behavior such as this is one way that children affirm their feelings of friendship for each other.

fun to team up with the threesome at a table having a tea party would do best to watch quietly for a few minutes. By remaining on the perimeter of the group, she has an opportunity to learn the rules of the game and to look for a suitable moment to enter the party. At a break in the play, she can sit down and begin doing whatever the others are doing — sipping imaginary tea, perhaps, or munching invisible cake. In a few minutes, if the club has not challenged her presence, she can affirm her membership in a more active way — passing out another piece of cake, for example. And, if all goes well, the cake will be received in the spirit in which it was offered, and the small coterie will expand to include another member.

On the other hand, a child who plunges directly into a group — or who calls attention to herself with questions and statements that do not match the activity at hand — is likely to meet with a quick rebuff. The instinct to exclude is strong in small children, and even when a youngster adopts the subtler strategy, she may be rejected on her first foray. Consequently, children need to develop not only the skills for entry but the resilience to spring back when met with dismissive behavior and to try again at a later time. Parents and caregivers should encourage the child to view this kind of rejection as a temporary event, dependent on circumstances rather than on a personal flaw.

Maintaining peer relations

When children are very young they do not play together for long periods: They become distracted or quarrel over a toy, or perhaps one toddler goes running off to find his mother. Even preschoolers tend to move rapidly in and out of groups, rather than sticking with the same entourage for an entire morning or afternoon. Gradually, as children gain experience with peers, they sustain social involvement for longer stretches and begin establishing ties among themselves, choosing favorite playmates.

To keep play going — or to keep a friend — a child must know how to be attentive and responsive to others. In situations where socially mature children are enjoying play together, such behavior seems to occur naturally: The youngsters smile and nod at each other and talk happily about what they are doing. In the early years, however, this is more often the ideal than the reality. Young children must learn to cooperate with each other, divide up tasks, take turns, and share equipment and control.

This kind of give and take is important to successful peer relations: A youngster who consistently demands that he choose the games and the rules is unlikely to find himself with many playmates. Conversely, the child who can go along with the suggestions of others — and assert his own wishes clearly as well — will have an easier time making and keeping friends.

Handling conflicts

Even in the happiest of friendships, conflicts do flare, especially among young children, whose desires are strongly felt and frequently are bluntly expressed. During the toddler and preschool years, these disagreements most often arise over toys or other objects. As children begin to acquire possessive feelings about playthings, they may resort to blows when they feel their rights are being challenged. In fact, in the early years, you may wonder if grabbing, hitting and pushing are automatic responses triggered whenever a child feels his territory is threatened. From trial and error, however, and with adult guidance, children learn that such abuse is rarely effective; and they discover that it hurts to be on the receiving end.

A far more positive approach to reconciling differences is assertive behavior, in which a child clearly expresses his feelings and rights but does not infringe on the rights of another youngster. After the first few rocky years of playing with other boys and girls, a child may have enough self-control to manage this kind of conduct. When children can talk openly about a disagreement, it tends to dismantle their aggressive impulses. Once feelings are aired, a compromise may be reached — a toy shared, perhaps, or a game set on a different course. Apologies for misbehavior, when appropriate, and a sense of humor also help cool down conflicts. If you can guide your child to learn these skills as he goes along, you will find eventually that your services as a mediator are less and less in demand.

By handing a toy truck to her son and accompanying the action with the words "it's your turn," this mother demonstrates how to share, a basic social skill. Then she encourages her toddler to practice the sharing behavior she has just modeled.

Helping your child learn skills

Young children, of course, vary widely in temperament and in their ability to handle the social challenges described above. Even a socially well-adjusted child may at times encounter a temporary roadblock in the path to friendly peer relations. If you feel your child is having problems with some aspect of social behavior, it is entirely appropriate for you to step in with some tactful parental assistance, demonstrating skills in which the child is weak and encouraging her to practice them with you. Before intervening, however, observe your youngster at play with other children for a short while. Note how she goes about initiating contact with other children, how she reacts in group play, what she does when conflicts arise. At the same time, you will get a feel for how other children conduct themselves in their peer relations.

A technique for coaching   Studies show that coaching is a very effective way to help a youngster acquire better social skills. A coaching session in social skills is a little bit like a football drill. First you demonstrate the technique; then you ask the player — in this case, the child — to practice; finally you offer feedback. Of course, you would never employ the high-pressure tactics of a football coach; rather, approach the session playfully, in a relaxed manner.

You probably will want to choose a quiet part of the day and keep the coaching session short. And, since a child is likely to be sensitive about her vulnerable spots, avoid trying to coach her immediately after she has encountered a social problem. Begin by casually mentioning the situation in which the child has shown some difficulty and discuss it briefly with her.

For example, perhaps you have observed that your youngster rarely gets a chance to choose an activity when playing with friends, because she is shy about speaking up. You might say you have noticed that the other girls always seem to be the ones who pick the games and tell her you have an idea of how she might get the others to play her favorite game. Then tell your child you are going to pretend to be her for a moment and demonstrate a sample of what she might say to the group: "After we finish hide-and-seek let's go to my house and do finger painting next," or perhaps, "We haven't played hopscotch in a long time; how many people vote for that one?" Explain to her why the approach you are suggesting works. Then, have her switch roles with you and practice asking directly for what she wants. She may be shy at first, so encourage her with smiles and enthusiasm. And be generous in praising her efforts.

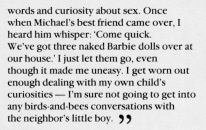

When Friends Come to Play

❝ Justin, who is three and a half, is still real worried about sharing his toys. When other children come to play, he seems to be excited at first. But then it's 'my train, my books, my blocks.' He doesn't seem to be able to enjoy company yet. Our latest tactic is to ask the play-mates to bring along something they can share. That sometimes helps the situa-tion. Justin is a lot better about sharing his stuff when he is playing with the other kid's laser pistols. **❞**

❝ Some kids just seem to have the wrong chemistry together. I encour-age Alice to invite certain friends over — the ones she plays with nicely. And I dream up all kinds of excuses about why she can't invite the others. I'm not sure whether that's fair, but I hate the way some of them play together. **❞**

❝ Five-year-olds bring out the worst in each other when it comes to bathroom words and curiosity about sex. Once when Michael's best friend came over, I heard him whisper: 'Come quick. We've got three naked Barbie dolls over at our house.' I just let them go, even though it made me uneasy. I get worn out enough dealing with my own child's curiosities — I'm sure not going to get into any birds-and-bees conversations with the neighbor's little boy. **❞**

❝ I always try to treat other kids exactly as I treat my own when they're playing at our house. But sometimes I do stop to think about it later — when I've had to get stern with the other person's child. I think I may be stricter than some par-ents are. What kinds of stories will those kids be carrying home? **❞**

❝ My five-year-old gets really bossy when her friends come to visit. Actually, she has been that way since she was tiny and worried about the other kids' playing with her toys. Now she and her friends are old enough to sense that being the 'guest' gives you special sta-tus and is something that you can take ad-vantage of. So there are still lots of ar-guments, since Meg wants to be the boss even though she's the hostess, too. My rule is that Meg has to let the guest choose the first game, then she gets her turn to choose the next. Children seem to obey other parents better than they obey their own, so I hardly ever have trouble with Meg's playmates. **❞**

❝ One big advantage with other peoples' children is that you always have the option of just sending them home if they start to give you any real trouble. You can't do that with your own — al-though sometimes I'd like to try. **❞**

In modeling social skills this way, you will need to be aware of your child's particular needs and level of understanding — and adjust your design accordingly. You do not need to go through every step every time. You might wish to weave your lessons into other kinds of play — with dolls or puppets, for example.

Once you think your child understands a new skill, remind her of it now and then, just before she is going to play with others. Children often simply forget that they have learned something, so you might casually say: "Remember the new way you learned to say you want to do something."

The power of positive reinforcement

When it comes to cultivating good behavior, an ounce of praise usually goes much further than an ocean of punishment. When your child behaves nicely to his playmates, make a point of letting him know that you are pleased. When you must criticize his conduct, try to keep your remarks positive and constructive. Finally, teach your child to praise himself for his social coups; when he triumphs over a difficulty, explain that he should give himself the proverbial pat on the back. ❖

The Role of Play Groups and Nursery Schools

By the time your child is two and a half to three years old, he probably will be ready for the stimulation that a play group or nursery school offers. In these environments, where a variety of children share space, equipment and adult supervision, the youngster practices his fledgling social abilities — and, as he associates with a wider circle, discovers new capabilities.

Social benefits

Perhaps the most valuable contribution a play group or nursery school makes to a child's education is the opportunity to mingle with children of different ages, cultures and personalities. This kind of social variety is hard to match at home. Furthermore, leaving the family nest has a maturing effect on most children. Without a parent nearby to arrange activities and smooth out conflicts, a youngster must tap his inner resources more often. His emerging confidence in his civilized self leads him to a greater sense of independence — which contributes to his enthusiasm for life in general.

Qualities to look for

Play groups and nursery schools vary in atmosphere, and you will want to choose a center that suits your child. It is often wise to select a social climate that complements the one a youngster has at home or in the neighborhood. For instance, a child with a wide circle of friends and several siblings could benefit from an intimate play group run by an attentive adult. On the other hand, a child who spends most of his time with parents and other grownups should have a chance to associate with a number of peers, relatively free from adult influence. Another consideration is your child's personality. A shy youngster may be overwhelmed in a large nursery school or with children who are mostly older than he, while a gregarious child could be stifled in a small group. Whatever your choice, look for features that promote positive social experiences: A diversity of children, adequate space and equipment, and caring and intelligent adult supervision are certainly musts. Be sure, too, that there is provision for children to play alone as well as with others, because few youngsters are happy socializing all the time.

The teachers or caregivers

The personality and style of the adults in charge have a significant effect on the social ambiance of a play group or nursery school. Look for caregivers who reinforce friendly, cooperative play with judicious amounts of attention and tactful encouragement. The adults should allow children plenty of social freedom but intervene when appropriate — to stop children from hurting each other or to help an isolated child join peers. ❖

Play That Teaches

A good nursery school or play group will provide an abundance of the kinds of toys and activities that promote socializing, in a way that is natural and fun. In general, any toy or piece of equipment that children can share will, at least some of the time, bring them together. Climbing bars, seesaws and other outdoor equipment are ideal, as are indoor materials such as train sets, dolls and building blocks. Toys that spark dramatic play — dress-up gear, for example, and props that suggest different settings — are also invaluable. In acting out real-life or imaginary situations, children practice such vital social skills as communication, taking turns and resolving conflicts. Many young children are especially drawn to toy kitchen appliances, brooms, beds and other miniature furniture, which they use to play house, creating their own fantasy home away from home.

The dramatic play that a game of dress-up inspires demands a high level of interaction. Children must discuss the details of setting and roles, and that requires both communication and cooperation.

Several preschoolers scramble about together on playground equipment, strengthening social skills as well as limbs. In outdoor play, children tend to be talkative and cooperative. As they chat, they may decide the structure is a house, a fire station or a tree in the forest.

Musical instruments bring a troop of children together for a common purpose (right), giving them a chance to practice taking turns in order to create something collectively. Adult organization is necessary for such activities; left to themselves, young boys and girls tend to play in smaller groups.

Even the classic little red wagon provides an opportunity for a few minutes of tandem play. Since one child pushes another, the sport gives some active practice in helping others and taking turns.

Balancing a number of building blocks to make a tower, the youngsters above discover that it is sometimes necessary to coordinate their actions very precisely in order to achieve a common goal.

With some behind-the-scenes advice from an adult, older preschoolers can stage a puppet show, an especially rich form of imaginary play. In discussing preparations, assigning roles and acting out scenes, the children exercise a broad range of social skills.

Developing Respect for People Who Are Different

At about the age of three, a child starts to discern that the world is made up of many people and that some of them are quite unlike himself. Almost every parent has experienced an awkward moment when the child makes a blunt observation about a difference he has suddenly noticed — in race, age or perhaps ability. Although potentially embarrassing, these candid remarks do not reflect any inherent prejudice. Usually they express curiosity or concern. Negative attitudes toward differences are picked up by impressionable young children from adults, other children and media stereotypes. Since a child's attitudes are shaped at an early age, teach him from the start to respect and accept others regardless of differences, so he will learn to appreciate diversity, rather than use it as a basis for judgment.

In addition to espousing open-mindedness, it is wise to expose your child to many different kinds of people, including those of contrasting cultures, various ages and a range of abilities. For such encounters, the most effective situations are those requiring active teamwork — such as a three-legged race or a joint building project; working together toward a common goal quickly helps break down the barriers imposed by differences, by focusing on how the people involved are alike.

Ethnic differences   How frequently your child meets children of other races and nationalities depends in large part on where you live. Some neighborhoods contain a mix of blacks and whites, Asians and Hispanics and other ethnic groups, while others are more culturally uniform. If your child tends to associate only with youngsters whose backgrounds are similar to her own, consider finding situations — at the local YMCA or community center, for instance, or at a nursery school or play group — where she will have a chance to experience a richer blend.

You can also help your child to develop a good attitude by reading books and watching television shows that portray people of every ilk in a positive light. And display a model of broad-mindedness yourself by treating all people respectfully, speaking out against racial or cultural slurs and, if possible, having a potpourri of adult friends.

No matter what you teach a child at home, however, she may one day announce her dislike for a playmate based on some cultural difference — an attitude that she is more likely than not parroting from another child or adult she has overheard. If this happens, simply remind her calmly that such differences are no cause to dislike a person. Redirect her attention to similarities between the other child and herself, perhaps pointing out games they both like to play, and explain again that differences help make other people interesting to know.

Older people Because many children have little contact with older people other than their grandparents, they may be shy with the generation beyond your own. Books, movies and television programs sometimes depict older people as helpless, eccentric or even mean — stereotypes that are often far from the truth. If the child has limited contact with older people, however, such images can shape his attitudes. Be sure to counter stereotypes by discussing them with your child, asking him to compare them to older people he actually knows. You might also provide an older child with books about vital, actively involved senior citizens.

In addition, look for ways to give your child positive experiences with older relatives and neighbors. One way to do this is to invite an older person along now and then on a family outing; another is to include a senior citizen among the child's babysitters. Not only do such opportunities teach the youngster to accept older people, valuing the contributions of age and experience, they help him adopt a positive attitude about aging. Finally, encourage your child to be patient with the slowdowns and frailties that may accompany old age; explain that they are a natural part of growing old, something that everyone, including him, may one day have to live with.

Age differences need not be a barrier to shared good times, as this boy and this woman discover by shucking corn together. From such enjoyable exchanges, a youngster learns to relate positively to older people.

Handicapped children Play between a handicapped and a nonhandicapped child benefits both youngsters. For the handicapped child, the opportunity to be with children who do not share his disability teaches him to get along in a world where handicaps are the exception rather than the rule, abetting his efforts to be self-sufficient. Sharing experiences with a nonhandicapped child also diminishes the sense of isolation a handicapped child can have. The youngster who does not have a disability learns to be comfortable with

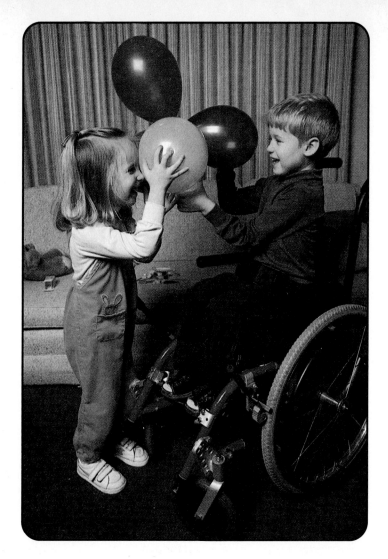

someone who does, looking beyond a physical or mental limitation to deeper human qualities and mutual interests.

Often the major obstacle is simply introducing a handicapped child into a group of nonhandicapped youngsters. Here, parents of the handicapped child may have to take the initiative, inviting other youngsters over to play or arranging an outing. Nursery schools and play groups also may bring the children together.

Since children — and their parents — may worry about hurting a handicapped child, or wonder what he can safely do, explain the child's abilities and limitations in a clear, matter-of-fact fashion. Being open about a disability makes it possible for everyone to understand and accept it. Even with the most skilled supervision, however, young children may tend to reject or shy away from a handicapped youngster in their midst. When this happens, the adult in charge should not try to force the children together but work patiently to involve them in a shared activity that will draw attention away from their differences. ❖

Special Situations

Every parent has occasion to worry about certain aspects of a child's social life. A friendship with a youngster of a different age, for example, may not conform to your ideal of peer interaction. You may be concerned when your child loses a friend, or if you find her talking earnestly with an imaginary companion. And few parents make it through their child's early years without encountering the youngster and a few friends engaged in the classic childhood game of playing doctor. Rest assured that in most instances, all of these situations are normal — commonplace markers along the road to social maturity.

Cross-age friendships

Associating with both older and younger playmates adds diversity to a child's social life and strengthens certain skills. As she plays with a toddler, for example, a preschooler will take on more responsibility than she ordinarily does with age-mates. She gives her leadership abilities free rein, liberated from the feelings of competition that sometimes plague children at the same stage in life. And, since a younger friend's needs are different from her own — and perhaps therefore more obvious — cross-age friendships cultivate empathy in the older child. Meanwhile, the junior partner in the twosome is learning to get along with a more forceful and mentally sophisticated friend, as well as benefiting from the older child's greater knowledge and experience. Just as important, cross-age friendships are mutually enjoyable: Toddlers love to romp with their tireless and inventive older friends, and the youthful admiration the little ones offer only encourages an older child's zest for play.

Two tricycle riders display the pleasures of friendships between children of different ages: smiling admiration for the younger one and pride in taking responsibility for the older youngster.

Friendships that dissolve

It is not unusual at all for friendships among children to shift rapidly and break up for one reason or another: Playmates disagree, outgrow each other, develop new interests and make new alliances just as grownups do. All the same, a child who loses a friend may feel sad, lonely and even angry for a time. A child who has been abandoned by a special friend is particularly apt to feel hurt and to need plenty of understanding and support from his mother and father.

Whatever the circumstances, allow the child to talk about his old friend freely, encourage him to see both the good and the bad in the friendship, and let him know that, although it ended, the relationship was valuable. As a parent, you should not rush your child through his feelings or try to push him into new friendships out of concern that he is at loose ends socially. Simply take the time to reassure your youngster that he will make a new friend in time, one who may be different from the old one but satisfying nonetheless.

When families move away

Loss of a friend who moves away, though a sad occasion, may not upset a child as much as personal rejection. Still, he may miss his playmate keenly. If this is the case, the child needs encouragement in talking about his old friend and time to establish new connections.

On the other hand, if it is your family that is moving, your child will face the loss of all his friends at once, and the very scary prospect of initiating many new relationships in unknown territory. There are some steps you can take to make things easier for him, beginning with helping him say good-by to his friends. The child may wish to bid them farewell at a festive gathering or prefer to do something special with each one. Keeping in touch through letters after you move can carry the child through the lonely period before he meets youngsters in your new neighborhood. While you do not want to pressure your child into this before he is ready, do provide him with opportunities to meet playmates — perhaps at a park, or in a play group or an organized youth program in your new community. Finally, be prepared for a temporary regression to less mature social behavior: An unfamiliar situation often raises social struggles you thought your child had resolved long ago.

Sexual exploration

Because sexual curiosity and feelings are normal in toddlers and preschoolers, you should not be surprised or alarmed if you come across your child half-dressed in some out-of-the-way spot, playing doctor with a friend. A child is naturally eager to explore his sexual feelings and to see what other children, of either sex, look like beneath their clothing. It is important not to make the child feel there is anything shameful about these feelings. Still, while there usually is nothing inherently harmful in children's playing doctor, it probably is not a game you will feel comfortable allowing to continue. Youngsters may

secretly appreci-
ate your calling a halt to their ex-
perimentation, too, since they often feel anxious and uncertain
about this kind of play.

A tactful suggestion that the children get dressed because it is
time to do something else is sufficient. You might propose an
intriguing activity as an alternative, then stay nearby to help the
children get started on the diversion. And, although you should
not punish or criticize your child for playing doctor, you could
suggest he ask you when he has questions about his body or
about the opposite sex.

Imaginary friends It is quite common for young children to invent imaginary
friends and creatures to keep them company, add excitement to
their lives and protect themselves from a world that can be
confusing and frightening. A child who fears large animals, for
example, may create a docile beast that submits to her commands, while a youngster who has lost a friend may bring forth
an invisible companion to relieve her loneliness. A child may
blame her imaginary friend when she herself misbehaves — pos-
ing a discipline dilemma for parents.

All of this behavior is perfectly normal and should be handled with patience and a sense of humor on your part. You
might even try addressing discipline to the invisible friend if
an occasion warrants correction. Minor irritations aside, as
long as your youngster has real friends as well, then you need not
spend time worrying about her make-believe ones. When the
child no longer needs the ally, the imaginary friend will somehow or other disappear from her life. ❖

*An audience of stuffed ani-
mals, creatures brought to
life by a little girl's imagina-
tion, listens attentively to her
talk. Small children often use
such companions as play-
mates and confidants.*

117

5 Putting Good Discipline to Work

As your child grows older and becomes increasingly involved in family activities and the society of other people, she should learn that good behavior encompasses a broad range of positive actions and attitudes beyond such simple basics as sharing toys and following rules. The well-behaved child will also have a sense of personal responsibility and social grace, which you can instill using the same principles of sound discipline that help discourage a youngster from misbehaving.

Watching, imitating and following your instructions, your toddler will gradually learn how to get dressed, feed herself and care for her own things. In the same way, she will learn how to be a contributing member of the household, helping out with simple chores and perhaps the care of family pets. If they are introduced in the right spirit, these lessons in responsibility will carry no trace of drudgery but instead will become her ticket to independence and greater control over her own life. She will take pride and pleasure in participating with other members of the family in daily tasks. And she will revel in the grown-up feelings of self-sufficiency that her new skills bring: Now, instead of wailing over spilled milk, she can sponge it up and proceed with her meal.

Your child's developing sense of responsibility will ultimately expand to include the pleases, thank-yous and other courteous gestures that help smooth relations with other people. The social approval she wins through good manners will boost her self-esteem and encourage her to continue behaving courteously. But your youngster's earliest lessons in manners, like all the other lessons of a young child's education, will be the examples her parents set at home and she observes.

The Road to Responsibility

With increasing physical skills and an emerging drive for independence, your toddler enters the "let me do it" stage of life and will happily want to join you in doing things around the house. You can help maintain his natural enthusiasm by bearing in mind the general principles about instilling responsibility that are discussed below. Above all, you need to keep all lessons on the light side; your role should be one of gentle guidance and encouragement, not drilling or nagging. Your primary goal is not to train a junior worker, but to show your child how things are done and allow him the fun of taking part.

Before your little one is old enough for regular chores, you can give him a feeling of usefulness by allowing him to help you spontaneously here and there. You might ask him to pick up a dropped spoon or bring you a piece of clothing from a chair; take care to praise him for his help. Even when you are engaged in a relatively complex job, there is usually some way for you to include him. If you are knitting, he might just hand you a ball of yarn and feel very good about being part of such an amazing project.

When you feel the child is ready to tackle a job of his own, make sure that the task you assign him, however simple, is a real one and not mere busywork. A youngster who helps set the table every day or who helps take the clothes out of the dryer feels proud to know that what he is doing is important to the running of the household.

Readiness for chores

Although your youngster can participate in many of your household activities from the time he is two, you should be careful to match the job to his skills. He will become frustrated and lose interest if you ask him to do something, even with your help, for which he is not quite ready. Most of the chores discussed here are rated by age to help you judge what to expect and when.

Teaching new skills to a preschooler takes time and practice, even when your youngster is ready and eager for the job. You might give him a sponge and a spray bottle filled with water when you are cleaning the kitchen and let him spray and wipe part of the counter while you do the rest of it. If you show your child patiently how to do a job and then work with him, he will learn to do it by himself while you watch. Eventually, the youngster will do it all by himself and take pride in a job that he has done on his own.

A child often is ready to move from simple to more complex tasks when he reaches a new developmental milestone; when he learns to count, for example, he can take from the drawer the right number of forks and spoons to be set at the table, rather than just having them handed to him. You will usually know when to add a new task. But if you misjudge your youngster's skills a bit and feel that it is necessary to lighten the responsibility, try not to make it seem like a punishment. Praise him for what he is able to do and explain, "We'll try the hard part again a little later."

Teaching a task step by step
It is a good idea to break a task down into small, manageable segments that can be explained in simple terms. Consider the counter-wiping exercise mentioned above: Simply asking a preschooler to "clean up the counter" is unlikely to produce a

successful result unless she has been shown each part of the process, starting with the stool she needs to reach the surface. She must be shown how to press the nozzle on her spray bottle to release the water and how to wet the sponge and wring it out in the sink so it will be usable. She must learn the wiping action with the sponge and how to push the crumbs into a pile, or into her cupped hand.

Each step of the task should follow in sequence, but do not fret if things get scrambled at first; remembering sequences is often difficult for a young child. And just when you think she has mastered the job, she may forget all or parts of it. If that happens, go on to something else for a while; you may be expecting too much too soon.

When she does master a job such as cleaning the kitchen counters, do not ask her to clean a bigger area than she can readily handle. Let her tackle a small section of the surface first, then gradually work her way up to doing the entire countertop. This step-by-step procedure applies to any job a youngster is learning — from picking up toys to keeping track of her backpack once she is going to and from school on her own.

Making sure not to litter the streets is an extension of this child's expanding sense of responsibility. A youngster who understands why he should tidy his room or clean up debris in his yard is not likely to be careless about disposing of candy wrappers or soda cans when he is outside.

A special time for chores

During his preschool years, your child learns to establish order in the physical world. Just as the idea of having an appropriate place for things becomes a part of his sense of structure, so does the notion of having an appropriate time for things. You may want to set aside a special period every day for work, or you may find it best to incorporate chores into the already existing mealtime, bathtime or bedtime routines. You might ask your youngster to set the table 20 minutes before dinner each night or to hang up the towels right after his bath.

While routines are important, you should leave room for flexibility. After your child has learned how to do a task, let him make some of the choices about it — which toys to pick up first, or which part of the counter to sponge.

The quality of the job

Eventually, you want your child not merely to learn a task but also to perform it well; she should develop her own internal standards and take pride in a job well done. But perfection is not important in the early years, and if you are too demanding too soon, you risk dampening the very enthusiasm you are trying to keep alive. Remember, there is plenty of time to perfect a task, and eventually she will learn.

You can encourage your little helper to begin thinking about standards by gently explaining what to look for after a task is completed. Show her, for instance, that the final step in wiping the counter is to hunt for any leftover crumbs or smears so as to be sure the counter is clean. You and she might make a "crumb hunt" together at first, so she can find the crumbs herself. Before long, she will be inspecting everything on her own before she reports the job done. While you are establishing inspection as the final step, you should be sure to let your youngster discover what is wrong and do the correcting; you will appear to lessen the value of her work by cleaning up the overlooked crumbs yourself.

Avoiding the stereotypes of gender

There is no need to think of certain tasks as suitable for boys and other tasks as proper for girls. To ensure that their youngsters will be able to take care of themselves as capably as possible in adulthood, parents are wise to introduce the whole range of household tasks to sons and daughters alike. Little boys enjoy making cookies and little girls like to rake leaves, and when they grow up they will feel both competent and independent by knowing how to cook and clean as well as how to take care of yardwork or change a washer in a faucet.

Incentives

Your toddler may need no further incentive for working than an invitation to join you in what looks like an interesting activity. But to sustain her enthusiasm, you should praise and encourage her for her efforts as well as for her achievements. "I'm glad you stuck to the job," you might say, or, "Seeing you try so hard makes me very proud of you." Do not wait until she learns to make hospital corners to laud her for helping you make the bed; an attempt to straighten the sheet should be enough to earn a hug in the beginning.

Using positive incentives to encourage desirable behavior is discussed on pages 46-49 of this volume. In addition to such motivating methods as work charts and special privileges, some parents give their child an allowance as an incentive for doing chores. Although there is much debate over this practice *(page 124),* most experts agree that an allowance can be a useful tool for teaching youngsters the value of money and how to make decisions regarding its use. ❖

Common Concerns

Children's Allowances

When is the best time to start giving a child an allowance?

While a few four-year-olds may be mature enough for an allowance, it is probably best to wait until the age of five or six. By that time, your child is starting to count and is ready to begin learning the names of coins and paper money. She has also learned that money can be exchanged for things. Before that, money does not mean much to children.

Should a youngster have to work for an allowance by doing chores around the house?

There is much debate about this. Some people feel that a child should earn his allowance by doing specific chores. But when an allowance is based on chores, the child may come to believe that he should receive money for all family cooperation, and he may be reluctant to do chores for which he is not paid. For this reason, many experts believe that an allowance should not be related to specific duties. Nevertheless, your child's contribution to the daily work of the family should be recognized and encouraged. You can explain that because he is a responsible member of the family who shares in the work, he is entitled to share in the family income and his allowance is his portion.

Should I use my son's allowance as a reward for good behavior?

Most experts feel that an allowance should not be doled out when a child is good or withheld when he misbehaves. Discipline for misbehavior should be tied more directly to the deed; an allowance seldom has anything to do with the child's good or bad activities, and withholding it will probably make little sense to him.

How much allowance should I give my five-year-old daughter?

In addition to her age, you will want to consider the community standards, what the allowance will be used to buy and your own economic circumstances. It is probably best to start with small amounts, but be realistic; consider the cost of an ice-cream cone or a

trinket from the toy store and decide on an amount that will enable your youngster to make purchases.

How often should an allowance be given to a child?

The norm seems to be once a week. Make sure you keep up your end of the bargain, paying your youngster consistently and on time.

Won't my child spend her money foolishly if I let her decide what to buy?

An allowance should be money the child may spend as she wishes. Parents may offer suggestions, but the point of an allowance is to teach your child to make decisions and learn the consequences of her choices. Let her learn the lessons for herself, even if she chooses a cheap item or trinket that you know will break the minute she gets it home. By living with her mistakes, your youngster will gradually learn to shop more carefully.

Should part of the allowance that I give my youngster go into a piggy bank for saving?

Parents can encourage thrift, but the notion of saving money for something in the distant future is beyond most five- and six-year-olds. At this age, children are learning to exchange money for goods and they need immediate gratification. As your youngster grows, you can explain that he may wish to save part of his allowance until he has enough money to buy something he cannot now afford. When you introduce the idea of saving, you should try to keep the waiting period short at first by helping your child set a small goal for himself.

My five-year-old has noticed that his eight-year-old brother gets a bigger allowance. Should I be giving the youngsters equal amounts?

Explain to your five-year-old that it is reasonable for an older child to get a bigger allowance. His eight-year-old brother has different expenses — school lunch or milk money, for instance. You might also say that youngsters always start off with a small allowance and that they then get regular raises, so it is only natural that you get more money as you grow older.

Household Tasks for Little Helpers

As soon as your child is old enough to understand what helping Mommy or Daddy means, you can begin to encourage her cooperative spirit. Start off by including her in whatever task you are doing in her presence. If you are making a salad, let her tear some lettuce; if you are setting the table, give her a napkin to put beside a plate. Before long, she will be a real help and will enjoy herself enormously, as well. As you look over the tasks that a preschooler is capable of doing, however, keep in mind that the main objective is not to save you work but to teach her skills and responsibility. In fact, having your child join you in the chores will probably increase rather than diminish your work load at first. But all the explanations and supervision will be worth it in the long run, when you wind up with a youngster who has learned how to share the family work load and has gained both competence and confidence in the process.

A row of hooks hung low on the wall of her room enables a five-year-old to hang up her book bag and clothing. Nearby is a hamper for her dirty clothes. Her well-organized room makes it easier for her to be tidy.

Taking care of possessions

From her earliest years, your child will pick up her toys to please you; but one day, she may start to put away her belongings because she finds tidiness satisfying for its own sake. She may feel good about taking care of them in the same way that washing herself imparts a sense of well-being. In order for her to reach this happy state, parents should make sure that positive feelings accompany each step of the cleaning-up process.

The first thing you can do to encourage orderliness is to organize your youngster's possessions so that they will be easy for her to care for. A low hook placed in or near the coat closet will encourage her to hang up her own coat; by the time she reaches the age of three she should be doing it on a fairly regular basis. Her toys should be arranged on a shelf where they are easily accessible and to which they can be handily returned. Shallow pull-out bins with a few toys in each also provide good storage; avoid the deep toy chest where playthings that find their way to the bottom seem never to surface again.

Your preschooler will undoubtedly own more toys than she can readily play with. Having large numbers of available toys to shuffle about can create confusion at cleanup time and may also tend to overwhelm her when she tries

Making her bed is part of this youngster's morning routine. The bed has been placed away from the wall to give the child easy access on three sides.

to choose what to play with next. So it is a good idea to keep only a few toys — probably a third of what she owns — on her shelves at any one time. As you rotate her toys, those most recently displayed will seem new. Of course, her favorites should be available all the time.

Tidying up together   You can help your youngster start taking care of her things by making it part of a playful, joint activity. "This end of the shelf will be your Teddy bear's home. Let's walk him to his house," you might tell your two-year-old. You can then suggest that she walk the Teddy bear home every day when she is finished playing with it. This may be enough to expect from a child so young; a year later, she might take responsibility for putting away another two or three toys on a regular basis.

It is important to explain just why things should be tidied up. Simply asking your toddler to put away her toys may not mean much at first. The place may look like a disaster area to you, but in your youngster's mind, the chaos may be colorful and comfortable. You will want her to know why the job should be done and that you will help her with it. You could say: "Some of your toys may get broken and a person could get hurt, so we have to pick up the toys. Let's do it together."

In this situation, breaking the job down into its separate elements is very helpful. "First, let's put the puppets on the shelf," you might suggest, and when that is finished, "Now we'll stack the blocks in the corner."

After a period of jointly picking up toys with your three-year-old, you can ask her to do it herself, provided you are in the room with her, pointing out each toy. A four-year-old can shelve most of her toys, but not in the orderly way she will have mastered the following year. She still will require some supervision, although it may be enough for her to call you when she has finished picking up her room and is ready for you to inspect the job. Then you can praise her for doing it so well. But it is best not to expect her to tidy the whole room by herself on a regular basis until she is about six.

Taking care of clothing and making the bed can be learned in a similar manner. Ask your toddler to help you pick up the dirty clothes on the floor and put them into the hamper, then gradually let her do it all by herself. There are bound to be questions about what is dirty and what is not. It is enough at first to assume that if they are on the floor they are dirty. Later, you can help her distinguish between what is ready for the laundry and what can be put away for another wearing. By the time she is four or five, she will be able to sort out her clothes and pick up without you. Practice at bedmaking can begin as early as three, when your child can pull up the bedclothes in some rough fashion. At five, she can learn to pull up the sheet, quilt and blanket and straighten the pillows with your help.

Make sure that taking care of her possessions is incorporated into your preschooler's daily routine. It is a good idea to tidy up at a set time each day, stressing: "First we make the bed, then we go out to play," "Every evening we put our toys away, then we wash our hands and go in to dinner," or "After we get undressed, we sort out our dirty clothes and put them in the laundry hamper."

Accepting responsibility for the task

Once a child understands a chore that has been assigned to him and has done it comfortably a few times, he needs to feel that he is responsible for it. Resist the temptation to pick up his Teddy bear if he is slow to do it; give him as much of a chance as possible to do it himself. This can be difficult; you will need to exercise considerable self-restraint to leave a toy on the floor when it is so easy to pick it up and put it away yourself. But if your youngster sees that you routinely pick up his Teddy bear, he may wonder why he needs to perform the task at all — and will let you do it every time. Try to establish the principle that the chore belongs to the child, just as the toy or shirt belongs to him; this should become clearer as he grows older and more possessive about his belongings.

If your child is in some kind of day-care program, you will want to determine whether this experience is having a positive or negative effect on your efforts to teach tidiness. A caregiver at home may be too quick

With a child-size broom, the toddler pictured above is learning to sweep the floor and gather the dust and debris into a pile.

to pick up after your child, and you may have to instruct her in the procedure you want her to follow. At a day-care center or in nursery school, on the other hand, your youngster is probably practicing every day the routines of neatness you would like to instill. Talk to the staff about it and make sure that you are supporting at home the discipline being developed at the center. On the other hand, if you find that the program at the center is not to your liking, you may wish to consider alternative day-care arrangements.

General household chores

As your youngster follows you around the house, let her play and imitate you. If you are dusting, equip her with colorful flannel cloths cut into washcloth-size squares. Point out where the dust collects and show her how to wrap the cloth around her fingers and wipe it away.

Your toddler may also want to help vacuum the floor, although some young children are afraid of vacuum cleaners because of the noise and may need extra reassurance. When your little one is very young, you can get her a toy vacuum to play with. Later, she will enjoy connecting the parts of the real vacuum cleaner. Show her how to turn it on and off; give her an area of the rug to clean and demonstrate how to run the machine back and forth. Make certain she understands that only an adult is allowed to plug the electrical cord into the outlet.

Helping sort the laundry is fun and gives your young one the chance to practice a wide range of emerging skills; she must recognize shapes as she differentiates one form of clothing from another, and she will practice her math as she counts the number of articles in each pile. It helps to be specific in the directions you give your child, such as: "Take all the socks and put them in this pile." She can also help you put the folded laundry back in the appropriate drawers. As she matures, the youngster may become dexterous enough to roll the socks and fold underwear and small towels.

At the supermarket, your toddler will undoubtedly help you pick out some grocery items, and when you return home, she can help you put them away. Place the bags on the floor and ask her to hand you the groceries, one at a time. Be careful of cans or cartons that may be too heavy, or of items that she might damage, such as tomatoes or eggs. Let her put a few things away on low shelves that she can reach.

All youngsters love to touch and rub, and cleaning silver, copper or brass can be a particularly satisfying task for your preschooler, as she magically makes the shiny metal emerge from its coat of dark, slippery polish. Set out one or two pieces of lightly tarnished silverware or other metal items on the counter beside the sink. Apply polish to a damp cloth and show her how to rub the object until it gleams brightly. If you do not like the idea of your young one touching actual polish, buy a pretreated polishing cloth and let her use that. In any case, avoid asking her to polish heavily tarnished pieces; very young children do not have the persistence to continue rubbing a single piece for a long time. After your child has polished an item, show her how to rinse and dry it.

Many youngsters feel especially useful and important if they are allowed to help care for younger siblings. It should be the child's choice, of course, and you should not push if she declines. But if she feels like it, she might help you dress the baby or assist in folding and putting away diapers. She will get a new perspective on bedtime by helping you put the baby to sleep; she may even want to sing the infant a lullabye or tell him a bedtime story, just as you do for her.

This kindergartner is helping make cookies by mixing and stirring the batter. With a little help, the child will be able to carry out the remaining steps in the recipe — and gain satisfaction from doing it herself.

Your youngster can participate in a variety of kitchen activities that he will be thrilled to call "cooking." One three-year-old, for example, announced proudly to his nursery school class: "I like to help my Daddy make breakfast so today I got my own banana."

The range of food-preparation tasks your toddler is capable of goes well beyond peeling bananas. He can wash vegetables; he probably will enjoy it more and do a better job if you supply him with a vegetable brush. He can make a peanut butter-and-jelly sandwich using a table knife, and he can practice his rhythmic coordination as he mixes eggs in a bowl. He will develop his spatial and artistic skills by arranging cheese slices on a tray and decorating them with olives or cherry tomatoes. Ground meat is interesting to work with, and most young children delight in molding and patting a meat loaf into shape.

A family obviously has to eat every day, and a youngster who has the job of setting the table on a regular basis knows that he is making an important contribution to family life. The earliest and simplest task for a toddler is putting out the place mats. Occasionally, you may want to use plain white paper ones and let him decorate one or more with crayons or markers. Or use a paper table-

Setting the table, which is a perfect task for pre-schoolers, teaches responsibility, along with providing impromptu lessons in sorting, matching, counting and shape recognition.

cloth that your little one has decorated.

To help him with the silverware, draw a picture on a paper place mat of how the spoons, knives and forks should look when the table is set. When your youngster is three, he can learn how to place the utensils over their pictures on the mat. Hand him one item at a time — first the spoons, then the forks and knives. Explain to him specifically, "Put one spoon at each place," pointing to the proper picture on the place mat. He may not get it right immediately, but eventually the child will learn — and his understanding of spatial concepts will be enhanced in the process.

Your child can also distribute napkins. At first you might want to put paper napkins in napkin rings to prevent these lightweight papers from dropping under the table as he attempts to place them by the plates. After he has developed greater finger agility, he can put the rings on the napkins himself.

An older preschooler can pour milk or juice from a pitcher into a cup or a glass. But first, you may want to let him practice by pouring small bits of a solid substance such as rice. Whether using liquid or rice, he should start with a small pitcher containing half of what the cup holds. When your child becomes adept at pouring, he can pour from a pitcher containing more than the cup's volume.

When dinner is over, you can ask your youngster to put his own dirty dishes in the sink or on the counter. He can also help you clear the table, handing you one dish at a time; let him start at his own place and go around the table in order. He might carry the silverware into the kitchen, a few pieces at a time. And it will be more like a game if you ask the youngster to clear the silverware off the table in categories — first all the forks and then all the spoons and knives.

Helping outdoors   A fine sunny day when the whole family is enjoying the outdoors together is a good time to introduce your toddler to outdoor chores. All children seem to enjoy activities that involve filling and emptying containers, so give your little one a bag and let him fill it with litter or grass cuttings and then empty it into the trash can. The youngster can also help clean up when you are out on a picnic; start by telling him to put his own paper plate and napkin into the trash can, then he can help you pick up whatever has fallen to the ground.

All children should learn how and where to put away outdoor toys such as balls, tricycles, bubble pipes or other equipment. Allow enough time for you and your youngster to complete these tasks before he has to come inside.

At four, your child can assist with the gardening, helping you weed or doing it himself while you supervise his efforts, and he can join you in planting seeds and watering them. He will feel very proud when he later helps you cut and arrange the flowers that grow as a result or helps pick the vegetables and wash them for dinner.

Most children love playing with water, and you can make a game of helping you wash the car. At the age of two, a youngster can wipe the car with a soapy sponge; an older child may be able to manipulate a long-handled window cleaner. Children of any age will want to splash the car with the hose. Just make sure that the weather is warm enough, and that your child's clothes will not suffer from getting wet.

So long as there are no streets for him to cross, an older preschooler will feel important running errands for you in your neighborhood, borrowing or bringing various objects or carrying messages. As he delivers the message or object, he will be developing verbal and social skills as well as a sense of responsibility. ⁘

Daddy's eager helper enjoys stacking the wood his father has cut. With each small job the youngster undertakes and completes, his confidence expands and groundwork is laid for bigger successes.

Caring for Pets

Having a pet can be an enormously enjoyable and instructive experience for your preschooler. Not only will he feel close to a particular creature or collection of them; animals can also broaden his sense of responsibility to include a powerful respect for all of nature, as well as his environment.

However, before you embark on an adventure in pet ownership, take a bit of time to consider your own attitudes. Do you like pets? Are you ready for the considerable amount of work it will take to teach a young child to care for one? If you are uncomfortable about certain pets or do not care for animals in general, you will be wise to forgo acquiring one. Do not get a pet for your youngster simply because "it is good for him." He is likely to absorb your negative attitudes, and you do not want him to have an unhappy experience.

But if pets are on your list of pleasures, you can proceed with confidence, so long as you bear in mind that pet care must be under closer parental supervision than some other activities. You will probably have to teach your toddler how to play with an animal, since he may not recognize when he is hurting it by an excess of affection. And you cannot expect a preschooler to manage the sole responsibility for feeding even a goldfish.

As in other instances of teaching responsibility, you should break each task down into small parts. Your three-year-old can fetch the cat's or dog's dish and watch while you fill it with food or water, then take the dish to the pet; after the first few times, he can help you fill the dish. By the time he is four, he can pour the food out himself and feed the pet when you ask him to. But even when he masters the job, you should not place the entire responsibility on his small shoulders. He may be an enthusiastic and devoted caretaker for the first few days, but after that, he is likely to be busy with other things and forget about it.

A child's attitudes and ability to interact vary with his age, which is an important consideration in shopping for pets. For instance, a large, fluffy dog or a sharp-clawed cat is inappropriate for a two-year-old, although either might make a splendid pet later on. For a younger child, the best choices are easy-to-manage pets that will fit readily into his small world.

This is one reason why a goldfish makes an excellent pet for a toddler, who will observe its motions with fascination and, in time, learn to feed it and clean its aquarium. At three, your youngster can help you measure out the food flakes, and by four, he can be measuring them out himself. Still, you should stay nearby and be sure he understands that little fish have little appetites and should not be given too much food at a time.

Lessons Learned from Animals

"We got Kirk two parakeets, thinking we could take them out of their cage and play with them. But they turned to each other for company and aren't that interested in any of us people. Kirk was disappointed at first. But now he's figured out that animals do what they want, and it may not always be what he wants them to do. And he sees there are other rewards in caring for the parakeets. Kirk enjoys watching them, and when he gives them pieces of apple, he likes the way the two birds make a lot of noise and rush at each other, fighting over the treat."

"After Amy learned to walk I began taking her along with me to walk our dachshund. I showed her how I used the pooper scooper and told her that it was the law in New York that you had to clean up after your dog. When we visited my mother, who lives in another city, Amy was horrified to see that the people did not clean up after their dogs there. 'You have a dirty city,' she told her grandma. And when it was my mother's birthday, Amy wanted to send her a pooper scooper."

"My daughter Lynn is an only child and has not had to make any adjustments to siblings, so it has been our dog, Drummer, that has taught her there are other living creatures whose needs have to be met as well as her own. For instance, she has come to understand that Drummer must be walked in the evening before she can have her dinner. She has also learned through the years what treatment Drummer will tolerate and how much she can safely bug him — just as she might have learned with a brother or sister."

"When our cat died of an illness, I let the vet's office dispose of the body. Our daughter Laurie was sad that we couldn't bury Muffy and it seemed she would never stop mourning. One day we went to visit my grandfather's grave and Laurie asked, 'Why doesn't Muffy have a gravestone like Grandpa?' It set me thinking, and I asked her to draw a picture of the cat. Then we wrote its name and the years it was born and died, and we hung the picture in a frame in Laurie's bedroom. After that Laurie began to talk about the cat in cheerier ways — and it seemed that she had finally put her grief to rest."

The older child may become bored by goldfish, and by the time he is five or six, you may wish to get an aquarium of multi-colored tropical fish, perhaps even a small breeding tank where he can observe the life cycle in miniature. Six is also a good age for your child to have his own gerbil, hamster or guinea pig, all of which are small and relatively easy to care for. But you still will have to remind him to feed his pet and help him clean its cage.

From time to time, you may find an opportunity to care for a wild creature, perhaps something you and your child come across in the garden: a newt, or salamander, or a frog or turtle. Such animals have specialized needs and often delicate constitutions. It is a good idea to consult an expert about feeding and habitat, and to explain to your child that the animal eventually should go back where it came from. Yet creatures from the wild can provide a memorable learning experience, teaching your child how to enjoy something for a period of time and then return it to its natural environment.

The Well-Mannered Child

Little Miss Manners, in her white lace gloves and best-dress finery, is surely not the everyday image of your preschooler knocking on a friend's door to play. And silver serving dishes and carefully knotted neckties will naturally be reserved for special occasions and holidays. Yet the basic principles underlying formal etiquette remain the same for all situations, and for people of all ages: Good manners essentially have to do with thoughtfulness and kindness toward others, and everyone needs them to get along happily in society.

Children are not born with the social graces. Your youngster will learn to act politely only if you patiently teach her how and — above all — provide the example. Toddlers do what their parents do, acting out the behavior that they see and hear at home. If you make a point of being mannerly to your child and to others, sooner or later she will reflect your courtesy in her own behavior.

In setting an example for your youngster, you will have to decide how far to go in saying "please" and "thank you." It may seem like overdoing it a bit to trowel on the politeness for every little thing, though you will want to instill the idea firmly. But whatever you do, be consistent — and be ready to acknowledge any significant lapse in your own manners. If you happen to snap peevishly at your toddler, do not be afraid to admit that there are more polite ways of expressing your feelings.

When your child is small, in addition to modeling good manners yourself, you undoubtedly will have to remind her many times to wipe her mouth with a napkin or not to speak with her mouth full. But keep it pleasant and try not to nag, lest she get stubborn. And be sure to reward courteous behavior with praise, just as you would any other learning success.

You can begin your earliest lessons in good manners as soon as your child starts to talk. At two years or even 18 months, a toddler can learn to say "please" and "thank you." When you give her a cookie, say "thank you" yourself and she may try to imitate your words. It is important from the start to send the message that politeness is important to you. However, it is also important to understand that the learning process will be gradual and will continue throughout childhood. As a rule, preschoolers cannot be expected to remember social conventions without prompting. At two or three years, your youngster will try to be mannerly not because she truly comprehends, but because it is expected of her and seems to please her parents. Even as she approaches school age, do not expect too much too soon. When your child is six, although she will have mastered some basic principles of courtesy, you will

still be laying the foundations for the more
polished manners that will follow in later years.

Table Manners

Teaching table etiquette is complicated by the
fact that toddlers are still perfecting the physical skills of eating with utensils, drinking from a
cup and using a napkin effectively. Another
problem is that some of our social conventions,
such as waiting for the cook to be seated before eating, run counter to the impulses of a small
child. As a result, most sit-down meals
throughout the preschool years will have to include an element of training. The trick is to
find a comfortable balance so that the lessons in
manners do not spoil the fun of eating together. Some children will be more mindful of their
manners if you introduce a note of formal-
ity — saying grace before you eat, perhaps, or
having candlelight on occasion.

   You will of course want to resist the impulse to teach all the fine points at once. Start
with a few simple rules: We do not start eating until the person serving the meal sits down.
We eat the food on our own plates only. We
remain in our seats until we are finished, then ask
permission to leave the table. By the age of
three, your youngster should be able to remain
seated for 10 or 15 minutes, although not for
much longer. About the same time, he will become proficient with a spoon and a fork, and
he can be taught to chew his food with his mouth
closed. In the months that follow, he should
learn to ask nicely for second helpings and can
start to practice serving himself from the plat-
ter. Keeping elbows off the table is a difficult lesson for some youngsters, especially smaller
ones who may be using their arms to stay balanced at adult-size tables.

   By four years of age — and sometimes sooner — your preschooler should be able to take
turns in mealtime conversation. Learning not to
interrupt will be hard. Your best approach is
to include your little one in the conversation and
thank him when he manages to wait his turn
to speak. Keep in mind that when he does interrupt, he is probably not being intentionally
rude; he simply has a short attention span. Usually, it will be up to you to keep the conversation flowing. Make it a rule that dinner is not the
occasion for arguments and try not to engage
in adult discussions over your child's head.

   Purposely rude behavior at the table may
occur around the age of four or five. Do not be
discouraged by such backsliding: It is merely
an attention-getting device and will pass. Console
yourself with the thought that your youngster
is making progress if he knows the rules well
enough to break them on purpose.

Dining Out

Going out to eat is a great adventure for most youngsters, although it can be a real challenge in the good-manners department. To help things go smoothly, you need a little forethought and preparation.

Since your toddler is bound to be a somewhat messy eater, it is probably wise to start by having lunch at a fast-food outlet or pizzeria, where you do not have to worry about someone else's plates, cutlery or tablecloths. As skills improve and confidence grows, you can step up to a more formal setting, perhaps a pancake house or a family restaurant.

One of the problems you will want to address at a table-service restaurant is the time it takes for the food to arrive. Waiting can be frustrating to youngsters, so you might want to choose a place where you know the service is relatively swift. In any case, you can help the situation by bringing along coloring books, small toys or perhaps a bit of finger food to tide your child over until the meal arrives. You can lay the groundwork for future dining-out courtesy by paying special attention to the waiter or waitress, pointing out to your child how hard such people work and how they deserve to be thanked for their efforts.

Whenever possible, schedule your restaurant visits at off-peak hours, when the service is likely to be quicker than normal and the personnel more likely to smile benignly at your young one's inevitable mistakes.

When Your Child Is a Guest

It is natural to want your child to be a little more formal and restrained in other peoples' homes than in her own. Most children seem to sense this and will cut loose in unbridled play only after they are fully comfortable in a foreign environment. When your youngster is going for a visit, remind her about manners but do not recite a long list of things for her to remember; just focus on the most important points.

If your child will be spending the night, remind her to keep her things together and not scattered all over the host's house. Some youngsters do better on this score if you get them excited about the process of packing their own overnight bag, especially if it is a small one they can carry themselves. Another point you may wish to emphasize is that your youngster should not displace things in someone else's house; for example, when she uses a towel, she should put it back on the rack where it was. Your child should learn that it is polite to knock on closed doors before entering, and to wait for an invitation to eat something instead of simply helping herself to food, drink or sweets. And she should by all means remember the magic words that will make her a welcome guest: "please," "thank you," "excuse me," "good morning" and "good night."

Telephone Courtesy

Most children are not really able to conduct a proper telephone conversation until they are about four years old. If you wish to spare callers confusion or frustration, discourage your toddler from picking up the phone when it rings. Later, when he is ready to answer calls, some rehearsal is probably in order. Practice with a toy phone or with the unit disconnected from the wall and establish a formula for what you want him to say: "Hello, this is the Browns' house," for example, or "Hello, this is Casey." Emphasize the need for him to speak loudly enough to be heard and to respond to yes-and-no questions verbally rather than with nods and facial expressions.

Your child may also need to be taught to avoid conversing with other people in the room while he is on the phone — a sure source of confusion for the person at the other end of the line — and to explain to the caller what he is planning to do before putting down the phone and running off to find Mommy. Your four- or five-year-old is perfectly capable of remembering simple messages, such as "Aunt Sally called." Alas, there is a likelihood that he will neglect to convey the message to you.

Thank-You Notes

The underlying point in teaching good manners is to get across the idea that other peoples' feelings are important. The practice of sending thank-you notes for gifts or special favors brings the lesson home even for children who are too young to write. Keep on hand a supply of blank postcards for your youngster and buy some stickers so he can personalize them. By the age of five he will probably be able to dictate the thank-you message for you to write out, and then he can print his name at the bottom. But even a three-year-old may — with a little prompting — be able to tell you the things he would like the note to say.

Be selective, however, in choosing occasions for thank-you notes. A polite note of thanks will be a meaningful exercise after Christmas gifts from faraway grandparents and friends or after an outing with the parents of a playmate. On the other hand, a thank-you note for each and every present received at a birthday party is unnecessary and will seem like drudgery; the thanks can be made at the party itself.

When Grownups Come to Visit

Parents differ in their outlooks about what children should do when there is adult company. Some enjoy seeing children at the center of things, interacting with the adults. Others prefer that the little ones remain out of the way, and in some cases they hire a sitter so that the children will receive adequate attention and care, leaving the adults free to enjoy themselves. Most mothers and fathers agree, however, that preschoolers should at least be taught to greet visitors politely and converse for a moment or two.

You should make a rule that the TV goes off and the toys are put aside while your youngster stands up to say hello. Even a toddler can perform the traditional handshake; she should also learn to look guests in the eye when they are talking to her and she to them. Occasionally, a child will try to ignore guests entirely, whether out of shyness or a genuine belief that the grownups will not see her if she simply walks by. Sometimes it is a revelation to a child if you tell her that even grownups can have their feelings hurt if she does not say hello. With a two- or three-year-old, you may need to rehearse greetings before visitors arrive, then coax her through a proper welcome at the door. Your four-year-old should show some initiative in welcoming guests, although she may need to be reminded of this duty.

To help your child learn to be sociable, especially in the presence of strangers, you should allow her to practice conversational skills in ways that are not overly taxing. Try to keep the socializing short and pleasant. Make her a part of the conversation, rather than the object of discussion. Lead the conversation by asking her specific questions, not vague, open-ended ones. Rather than asking your youngster to describe what she is doing at day care, you might say something like this: "Jenny is learning about dinosaurs now. What did you say your favorite one was, Jenny?" To help her learn the art of conversation, you can gently draw her out in this fashion, but you may also have to do some of the talking for her, modeling the ways that she might tell her own stories.

When a child commits a faux pas before guests, it usually is best to wait and discuss it in private. Likewise, resist the impulse to scold a child for being forthright or even brutally frank in conversation — even if her comments are embarrassing. You might wish to mention it later. But preschoolers cannot be expected to have well-developed sensitivities about what observations to keep to themselves.

Party Manners

For all their fun and excitement, birthday parties can be unsettling to your preschooler. Being suddenly thrust into a group of other boys and girls his age — some of them, perhaps, strangers — may make him feel threatened and cause him to forget his manners. At the very least, it will test all the social graces you have been working to teach him. The youngster will have to ask for things nicely, remember to say thank you, be polite at the table and work at making somebody else feel special.

It may be even more stressful when the birthday is his and he is the guest of honor. Indeed, his birthday party may be the first time that the youngster has played host to more than one or two other children. Many young children are simply overwhelmed by the combination of heightened expectations and being the center of attention.

You can help your child prepare for such a social challenge by going over all the points of etiquette he has been practicing. But you should be realistic about what to expect, particularly if he is the birthday boy. In fact, it is not uncommon for the star of the show to be the worst behaved youngster at the party. This is particularly true of toddlers but often holds for older children as well.

As you get your youngster ready for the party, try to give him a concrete idea of what will happen and when. Most children will eagerly throw themselves into a full-fledged rehearsal for their celebration, especially if you make it fun. Play-act the young host's role at the party, paying attention to all the social amenities you would like to see him observe. Give special emphasis to the polite way of greeting guests.

You can school him to open his presents gracefully and not rip away the wrappings with a whoop, but this will be very difficult for him to remember. And be sure to alert him that his guests will want to try out his new toys. Urge him to do his best to share and remind him that once the guests are gone, the toys will be his alone. Even if the youngster does not rise to the occasion the day of the party, the days leading up to the big event should have been productive in terms of learning manners.

In addition to putting your child through rehearsals, do all the planning and preparation you can to make the event go smoothly. Above all, you should keep the party small in number and short in duration. When the big day arrives, be tolerant of lapses in social grace — and be especially generous with praise if your child's manners shine.

Bibliography

BOOKS

Ackerman, Paul R., and Murray M. Kappelman, M.D., *Signals: What Your Child Is Really Telling You.* New York: Dial Press, 1978.

Ames, Louis Bates, with Carol Chase Haber and The Gesell Institute of Human Development, *He Hit Me First: When Brothers and Sisters Fight.* New York: Dembner Books, 1982.

Asher, Steven R., and John M. Gottman, *The Development of Children's Friendships.* New York: Cambridge University Press, 1981.

Baker, Bruce, et al., *Behavior Problems.* Champaign, Ill.: Research Press, 1976.

Bisschop, Marijke, and Theo Compernolle, *Your Child Can Do It Alone.* Englewood Cliffs, N.J.: Prentice-Hall, 1981.

Blechman, Elaine A., *Solving Child Behavior Problems: At Home and at School.* Champaign, Ill.: Research Press, 1985.

Brenner, Barbara, *Love and Discipline.* New York: Ballantine Books, 1983.

Cherry, Clare, *Please Don't Sit on the Kids: Alternatives to Punitive Discipline.* Belmont, Calif.: David S. Lake, 1983.

Chess, Stella, M.D., Alexander Thomas, M.D., and Herbert G. Birch, M.D., *Your Child is a Person: A Psychological Approach to Parenthood without Guilt.* New York: Viking Press, 1965.

Christophersen, Edward R., *Little People: Guidelines for Common Sense Child Rearing.* Shawnee Mission, Kans.: Overland Press, 1977.

Clark, Lynn, *SOS! Help for Parents.* Bowling Green, Ky.: Parents Press, 1985.

Clemes, Harris, and Reynold Bean, *How to Teach Children Responsibility.* Los Angeles: Prince/Stern/Sloan, 1986.

Crary, Elizabeth, *Without Spanking or Spoiling.* Seattle: Parenting Press, 1979.

Dinkmeyer, Don, and Gary D. McKay, *The Parent's Handbook: Systematic Training for Effective Parenting.* Circle Pines, Minn.: American Guidance Service, 1982.

Dobson, James, *The Strong-Willed Child: Birth through Adolescence.* Wheaton, Ill.: Tyndale House, 1985.

Dodson, Fitzhugh, *How to Discipline With Love: From Crib to College.* New York: New American Library, 1979.

Dreikurs, Rudolf, M.D., *The Challenge of Child Training.* New York: Hawthorn Books, 1972.

Durrell, Doris E., *The Critical Years.* Oakland: New Harbinger Publications, 1984.

Eimers, Robert, and Robert Aitchison, *Effective Parents/Responsible Children: A Guide to Confident Parenting.* New York: McGraw-Hill, 1977.

Essa, Eva, *Practical Guide to Solving Preschool Behavior Problems.* Albany, N.Y.: Delmar Publishers, 1983.

Forehand, Rex L., and Robert J. McMahon, *Helping the Noncompliant Child.* New York: Guilford Press, 1981.

Fraiberg, Selma H., *The Magic Years.* New York: Charles Scribner's Sons, 1959.

Hainstock, Elizabeth G., *Teaching Montessori in the Home.* New York: Random House, 1968.

Halbert, Barbara Lee, *Creative Discipline for Young Children.* Nashville: Broadman Press, 1976.

Hoffman, Martin L., and Lois Wladis Hoffman, eds., *Review of Child Development Research.* Vol. 1. New York: Russell Sage Foundation, 1964.

Hunter, Madeline C., and Paul V. Carlson, *Improving Your Child's Behavior.* Glendale, Calif.: Bowmar, 1971.

Ilg, Frances, M.D., Louise Bates Ames and Sidney M. Baker, M.D., *Child Behavior.* New York: Harper & Row, 1981.

Isaacs, Susan, *Who's in Control? A Parent's Guide to Discipline.* New York: Perigee, 1986.

Kelly, Jeffrey, *Solving Your Child's Behavior Problems.* Boston: Little, Brown, 1983.

Kelly, Marguerite, and Elia Parsons, *The Mother's Almanac.* Garden City, N.Y.: Doubleday, 1975.

Kempe, Ruth S., and C. Henry Kempe, *Child Abuse.* Cambridge: Harvard University Press, 1978.

Kersey, Katharine C.:
The Art of Sensitive Parenting. Washington: Acropolis Books, 1983.
Helping Your Child Handle Stress. Washington: Acropolis Books, 1986.

Kopp, Claire B., and Joanne B. Krakow, *The Child: Development in a Social Context.* Reading, Mass.: Addison-Wesley, 1982.

Krumboltz, John D., and Helen Brandhorst Krumboltz, *Changing Children's Behavior.* Englewood Cliffs, N.J.: Prentice-Hall, 1972.

Lamb, Michael E., ed., *Social and Personality Development.* New York: Holt, Rinehart and Winston, 1978.

Lewis, Michael, and Leonard A. Rosenblum, eds., *Friendship and Peer Relations.* New York: John Wiley & Sons, 1975.

Lickona, Thomas, *Raising Good Children.* New York: Bantam Books, 1983.

McCullough, Bonnie Runyan and Susan Walker Monson, *401 Ways to Get Your Kids to Work at Home.* New York: St. Martin's Press, 1981.

Martin, Judith, *Miss Manners' Guide to Rearing Perfect Children.* New York: Atheneum, 1984.

Miller, Gordon Porter, and Bob Oskam, *Teaching Your Child to Make Decisions.* New York: Harper & Row, 1984.

Moore, Shirley G., and Catherine R. Cooper, eds., *The Young Child.* Vol. 3 of *Reviews of Research.* Washington: National Association for the Education of Young Children, 1982.

Mussen, Paul Henry, et al., *Child Development and Personality.* New York: Harper & Row, 1984.

Mussen, Paul, and Nancy Eisenberg-Berg, *Roots of Caring, Sharing, and Helping.* San Francisco: W. H. Freeman and Company, 1977.

Nelsen, Jane, *Positive Discipline.* Fair Oaks, Calif.: Sunrise Press, 1981.

Reit, Seymour V., *Sibling Rivalry.* New York: Ballantine Books, 1985.

Riley, Sue Spayth, *How to Generate Values in Young Children.* Washington: National Association for the Education of Young Children, 1984.

Roedell, Wendy Conklin, Ronald G. Slaby and Halbert B. Robinson, *Social Development in Young Children.* Monterey, Calif.: Brooks/Cole, 1977.

Rubin, Zick, *Children's Friendships.* Cambridge: Harvard University Press, 1980.

Scarr, Sandra, Richard A. Weinberg and Ann Levine, *Understanding Development.* New York: Harcourt Brace Jovanovich, 1986.

Schaefer, Charles E., *How to Talk to Children about Really Important Things.* New York: Harper & Row, 1984.

Schulman, Michael, and Eva Mekler, *Bringing Up a Moral Child.* Reading, Mass.: Addison-Wesley, 1985.

Segal, Julius, and Zelda Segal, *Growing Up Smart & Happy.* New York: McGraw-Hill, 1985.

Silberman, Melvin L., and Susan A. Wheelan, *How to Discipline without Feeling Guilty.* Champaign, Ill.: Research Press, 1980.

Stocking, S. Holly, Diana Arezzo and Shelley Leavitt, *Helping Kids Make Friends.* Allen, Tex.: Argus Communications, 1980.

Turecki, Stanley, M.D., and Leslie Tonner, *The Difficult Child.* New York: Bantam Books, 1985.

Wagonseller, Bill R., and Richard L. McDowell, *You and Your Child: A Common Sense Approach to Successful Parenting.* Champaign, Ill.: Research Press, 1979.

Wolfgang, Charles H., *Helping Aggressive and Passive Preschoolers through Play.* Columbus, Ohio: Charles E. Merrill, 1977.

Wyckoff, Jerry, and Barbara C. Unell, *Discipline without Shouting or Spanking.* New York: Meadowbrook Books, 1984.

PERIODICALS

Esposito, Beverly G., and Walter J. Peach, "Changing Attitudes of Preschool Children Toward Handicapped Persons." *Exceptional Children,* January 1983.

Esposito, Beverly G., and Thomas M. Reed II, "The Effects of Contact with Handicapped Persons on Young Children's Attitudes." *Exceptional Children,* November 1986.

Haswell, Karen L., Ellen Hock and Charles Wenar, "Techniques for Dealing with Oppositional Behavior in Preschool Children." *Young Children,* March 1982.

Honig, Alice Sterling, "Compliance, Control, and

Discipline." *Young Children,* January 1985.

McCall, Robert, "I Won't! And You Can't Make Me!" *Parents,* October 1984.

Miller, Cheri Sterman, "Building Self-Control: Discipline for Young Children." *Young Children,* November 1984.

Oden, Sherri, and Steven R. Asher, "Coaching Children in Social Skills for Friendship Making." *Child Development,* 1977.

Sander, Joelle Hevesi, "A Child's Role in the Family." *Parents,* May 1985.

Schoyer, Nancy L., "Divorce and the Preschool Child." *Childhood Education,* September/October 1980.

Schuman, Wendy, "Bad Problems/Good Solutions: Behavior-Modification Techniques to Help Parents Cope with Uncooperative Kids." *Parents,* October 1985.

Segal, Julius and Zelda, "The Power of Peers." *Parents,* July 1986.

Silvern, Steven, "Old and Young Together: Effect of an Educational Program on Preschoolers' Attitudes toward Older People." *Childhood Education,* January/February 1986.

Theroux, Phyllis, "Minding Our Manners." *Parents,* December 1986.

Weinstein, Grace W., "My Own Money." *Parents,* November 1986.

OTHER PUBLICATIONS

Cohn, Anne H., and Thomas Gordon, "Tips on Parenting." Chicago: National Committee for Prevention of Child Abuse, no date.

Forehand, Rex, Nicholas Long and Robert Wahler, "Outpatient Assessment and Treatment of Children's Behavioral and Emotional Disorders." Workshop presented at the Rivendell Conference for Clinical Practitioners, Memphis, December 1986.

Fried, Hilda, ed., "Plain Talk about Raising Children." Rockville, Md.: U.S. Department of Health, Education, and Welfare, no date.

Gordon, Thomas, "What Every Parent Should Know." National Committee for Prevention of Child Abuse, 1985.

Hayden, Alice H., et al., "Mainstreaming Preschoolers: Children with Learning Disabilities." Stock Number 017-092-00035-9. Washington: GPO, 1980.

Kieran, Shari Stokes, et al., "Mainstreaming Preschoolers: Children with Orthopedic Handicaps." Stock Number 017-092-00034-1. Washington: GPO, 1981.

Long, Nicholas, and Rex Forehand, "The Effects of Parental Divorce and Parental Conflict on Children: An Overview." Kansas City, Kans.: University of Kansas Medical Center, no date. Photocopy.

May, Gary, "Child Discipline: Guidelines for Parents." National Committee for Prevention of Child Abuse, 1984.

National Association for the Education of Young Children, "Helping Children Learn Self-Control: A Guide to Discipline." Washington, 1986.

Acknowledgments and Picture Credits

The index for this book was prepared by Louise Hedberg. The editors also thank: Kathern Bond, The American Humane Association, Denver; Christine Burger, Project for the Study of Young Children, George Mason University, Fairfax, Va.; Marguerite Kelly, Washington; Nicholas Long, University of Kansas Medical Center, Kansas City, Kans.; Barbara Lonnborg, Father Flanagan's Boys' Home, Boys Town, Neb.

The sources for the photographs in this book are listed below, followed by the sources for the illustrations. Credits from left to right are separated by semicolons; from top to bottom by dashes.

Photographs. Cover: Susie Fitzhugh. 7: Elyse Lewin/The Image Bank. 10-28: Beecie Kupersmith. 33: Susie Fitzhugh. 46-56: Beecie Kupersmith. 61: Elyse Lewin/The Image Bank. 93: Suzanne Szasz. 108: Nancy Blackwelder. 110: Pat Lanza Field; Elyse Lewin/The Image Bank. 111: Pat Lanza Field — Beecie Kupersmith (3). 114: Taisie Berkeley Trout. 119: Beecie Kupersmith. 121: Jim Cronk/Photographic Illustrations. 124: Beecie Kupersmith. 133: Suzanne Szasz. 134-139: Nancy Blackwelder.

Illustrations. 8: Marguerite E. Bell from photo by Bill Binzen/Photo Researchers. 9-14: Marguerite E. Bell from photos by Beecie Kupersmith. 16: Marguerite E. Bell from photo by Neil Kagan. 17: Marguerite E. Bell from photos by Beecie Kupersmith. 19, 20: Marguerite E. Bell from photos by Pat Lanza Field. 21: Marguerite E. Bell from photo by Suzanne Szasz. 22: Marguerite E. Bell from photo by Beecie Kupersmith. 23: Marguerite E. Bell from photo by Pat Lanza Field. 25-31: Marguerite E. Bell from photos by Beecie Kupersmith. 36, 37: Jack Pardue from photos by Beecie Kupersmith. 38, 39: William Hennessy Jr. 40: Jack Pardue from photo by Jean Shapiro. 41-43: Jack Pardue from photos by Beecie Kupersmith. 45: Jack Pardue from photo by Jean Shapiro. 48: Jack Pardue from photo by Beecie Kupersmith. 49: Gail Prensky. 52, 53: Jack Pardue from photos by Jean Shapiro. 55, 58: Jack Pardue from photos by Beecie Kupersmith. 63, 64: Donald Gates from photos by Beecie Kupersmith. 66: Donald Gates from photo by Vivian Ronay Barry. 67: Donald Gates from photo by Jean Shapiro. 70: Donald Gates from photo by Beecie Kupersmith. 71: Donald Gates from photo by Jean Shapiro. 73-75: Donald Gates from photos by Vivian Ronay Barry. 76, 77: Donald Gates from photos by Beecie Kupersmith. 78, 79: Donald Gates from photos by Vivian Ronay Barry. 81, 82: Donald Gates from photos by Beecie Kupersmith. 83: Donald Gates from photo by Vivian Ronay Barry. 84: Donald Gates from photo by Jean Shapiro. 85, 87: Donald Gates from photos by Vivian Ronay Barry. 88: Donald Gates from photo by Jean Shapiro. 89, 90: Donald Gates from photos by Vivian Ronay Barry. 95: Kathe Scherr from photo by Beecie Kupersmith. 96-100: Kathe Scherr from photos by Suzanne Szasz. 102: Kathe Scherr from photo by Bruce Roberts/Photo Researchers. 104-113: Kathe Scherr from photos by Beecie Kupersmith. 115: Kathe Scherr from photo by Lawrence Manning/West Light. 117: Kathe Scherr from photo by Beecie Kupersmith. 122: William Hennessy Jr. from photo by Nancy Blackwelder. 125: William Hennessy Jr. from photo by Pat Lanza Field. 126: William Hennessy Jr. from photo by Susie Fitzhugh. 127: William Hennessy Jr. from photo by Suzanne Szasz. 129: William Hennessy Jr. from photo by Pat Lanza Field. 130: William Hennessy Jr. from photo by Beecie Kupersmith. 131: William Hennessy Jr. from photo by Jim Cronk/Photographic Illustrations.

Index